COSMIC DANCES

of

THE ZODIAC

The star world now is flowing,
As living, golden wine,
Its joys on us bestowing,
Ourselves as stars will shine.

(Novalis)

CHOREOCOSMOS

SCHOOL OF COSMIC AND SACRED DANCE

Cosmic Dances of the Zodiac

Lacquanna Paul and Robert Powell

SOPHIA FOUNDATION PRESS

SAN RAFAEL, CALIFORNIA

THE SOPHIA FOUNDATION OF NORTH AMERICA

3143 Avalon Court
Palo Alto, California 94306, USA

Telephone/Fax 650-494-9900
Email: sophia@sophiafoundation.org
Website: www.sophiafoundation.org

Second edition, 2007
Sophia Foundation Press
An imprint of Sophia Perennis
© 2003 Lacquanna Paul and Robert Powell

Companion volume to *Cosmic Dances of the Planets*

For information, address:
Sophia Foundation Press, P.O. Box 151011
San Rafael, California 94915

Library of Congress Cataloging-in-Publication Data

Powell, Robert.
  Cosmic dances of the Zodiac / Lacquanna Paul, Robert Powell.—2nd ed., rev. & enl.
    p. cm.
  Includes bibliographical references.
  ISBN 1-59731-151-0 (pbk. : alk. paper)
  1. Zodiac. 2. Dance. I. Paul, Lacquanna. II. Title.

BF1726.P675 2006
133.5'2—dc22

                                        2006033170

CONTENTS

Cosmic *Eurythmy*
"In the image and likeness…"

Introduction: Study Material

The following work has been prepared as a guide and format for learning the twelve cosmic dances which celebrate the creative streaming of the zodiacal constellations. The forms and patterns of movement are described and illustrated so that their purpose and inspiring archetype can be readily grasped and understood.

In addition, there is recommended meditative work that can be taken up depending on the time available.

Legends and myths have existed throughout the ages concerning this greater macrocosm of which we are a part and which serves as an archetypal pattern for the forming of the human being. These stories provide an enrichment for our imagination and help to draw us more deeply into a conscious understanding and connection with the living currents (*life body*) of the cosmos, which holds the past as well as the future in a continuum of harmonic wisdom and order.

Through the images we can begin to behold the cosmic realm as a *relational field,* a rhythmic constancy of archetypal pattern (*space*) and purposeful movement (*time*) which draws us ever closer to the divine purpose of the future.

Astronomical and scientific findings and information are included as well as other material which has been formulated through observable phenomena over many hundreds of years. This information is offered as an enrichment to help deepen the cosmic dance material.

Research from the scientific findings of Robert Powell regarding the dating of the life of Jesus Christ as a mirroring of the wisdom of the stars has been woven into the text as well as the teachings of Rudolf Steiner concerning the cosmic unfoldment of Earth Evolution.

This material is intended as a *seed* to help *ferment* the process of discovery in finding a *relationship* to the archetypes of the twelve signs of the zodiac. The experience of cosmic dance works toward the forming of community. Thus, conversation and dialogue relating to the experiential discoveries of the participants in the zodiacal dances can be most fruitful.

Taken as a whole, through the movement of the dance which requires the engagement of the *will*, the experience of the music which addresses the *feeling* life, and the interactive nature of the discussion time which stimulates the *thinking*, one is brought into an awareness of the beauty, wonder, and magnificence of our human *relationship* with the cosmic realm of our spiritual origin – a relationship that may be experienced on a physical, soul and spiritual level.

Musical Accompaniment
"Dance only that music which goes from the soul in mounting circles." Isadora Duncan

The accompanying music for each of the forms has been chosen from the works of the great composers whose music reflects the inspiration of the *harmony of the spheres*. The music has been selected according to the corresponding key and rhythmical form or pattern of each of the twelve zodiacal dances. The mood of the music chosen for each sign of the zodiac objectively embodies something of the quality of the sign.[1]

Whenever possible, the dances should be accompanied by *live music* (piano or violin) since the etheric "vibrational quality" of the music is a potent and valuable aspect of the eurythmic experience, which brings about an enhancement of the flow of cosmic life forces.

However, when *live music* is not possible, a CD has been created by concert pianist Ludmila Gricenko. The "Zodiac Music" CD can be used for individual practice and (when necessary) for teaching in a group.

Instructions concerning the use of this CD are included in the Afterword of the teaching/study materials.

Eurythmy and Cosmic Dance
The cosmic dances work solely with the zodiacal gestures given by Rudolf Steiner, the founder of eurythmy. On the basis of his highly developed faculty of clairvoyance, Rudolf Steiner was able to perceive objectively the archetypal cosmic gestures of the signs of the zodiac, which he communicated in his lectures <u>Eurythmy as Visible Speech</u> in 1924. The sounds corresponding to the zodiacal signs are the *consonants* (and the vowel sounds of language correspond to the planets).

Not only does each zodiacal sign have an archetypal cosmic gesture but also a corresponding <u>sound</u> for which there is a eurythmic gesture. These twelve gestures are described in the following material as central to the twelve cosmic dances of the zodiac. Whenever reference is made to the sound of a zodiacal sign, this does not mean to vocalize the sound. (In eurythmy one does not vocalize the sounds at all.) Rather, it means forming the *gesture* of the sound. By not speaking the sound, a greater intensity of expression goes into the gesture expressing the sound *silently through movement*.

In the cosmic eurythmy we can experience that each of these gestures activates an *inner response* which works toward the strengthening of the human being and toward a greater alignment with the divine influences of the cosmic archetypes. To become conscious of this inner *formative* response is one of the goals of the Choreocosmos School. This is the healing aspect of the cosmic dance activity, which can be likened to the building up of Solomon's temple. The *creative* potency of each sound and gesture *speaks* within the participants as the human physical body becomes a *vessel* for the temple of wisdom.

---

[1] See the Afterword for a deeper discussion of this theme.

In the cosmic eurythmy participants learn to *sculpt* the gestures and sounds into the atmosphere of the surrounding space. This requires a cultivated awareness of the living substance of the etheric body of the earth. This awareness is cultivated through developing the capacity of inner silence and the activity of appreciation and love for the environment. This creates an attracting of life *substance* which is then shaped by the participants as a *blessing* for the surroundings and a *breathing back* to the spiritual world.

The choreographies for the twelve signs of the zodiac used in the cosmic dances have been developed by Robert Powell on the basis of the astronomical glyphs for the signs. (As mentioned below, the glyphs are derived directly from the zodiacal constellations into which the signs are embedded.)

The music accompanying the choreographies is in the musical key corresponding to each sign, so that the whole (music, choreographic movement, zodiacal gestures and gestures of the zodiacal sounds) weaves together in the sense of a *total work of art* capable of engaging one's whole being and leading one to a spiritual experience of these great cosmic archetypes.

The cosmic dances are thus a special development arising from eurythmy, concentrating solely upon <u>cosmic eurythmy</u>. The Choreocosmos School and the teachers of cosmic dance acknowledge their profound gratitude to Rudolf Steiner for bringing eurythmy into the world, thus creating a path – through movement – of coming to an experience of the cosmic archetypes of music and language and of the cosmic archetypes themselves. A more detailed description of the relationship of the cosmic dances to eurythmy, going more deeply into these interconnections, has yet to be written.

Important Reference Points for the Study Materials

The Sidereal Zodiac and the Zodiacal Signs

The purpose and design of the Cosmic Dance material is to provide the participants with an actual *experience* of the living cosmos. Therefore all references to the zodiac are in terms of the <u>sidereal zodiac</u>.[2] It is called the sidereal zodiac because it is based on the stars (Latin for star: *sidus, sideris*) as they actually appear in the night sky.

In the sidereal zodiac the twelve signs are defined in relation to the stars comprising the corresponding zodiacal constellations. The <u>scientific</u> definition of the zodiacal signs originated with the Babylonians who, in the world's first star catalog, specified the locations of the stars in each of the signs (Aldebaran at 15°Taurus, Antares at 15°Scorpio, etc.).

---

[2] The sidereal zodiac is the original zodiac of the Babylonians, Egyptians, Greeks, Romans, and Hindus. The sidereal zodiac was used by astronomers and astrologers for almost one thousand years before it became replaced by the tropical zodiac used in Arabic astrology, which was then introduced into Europe in the twelfth century AD. By and large it is the tropical zodiac that is used in modern astrology, with the exception of Hindu (Vedic) astrology that continues to use the sidereal zodiac.

6

The *signs* are literally <u>embedded</u> in the zodiacal constellations. And the eurythmy forms for the cosmic dances of the zodiac are based directly on the zodiacal signs. For example, on page 19 the zodiacal sign of Taurus ($\bouncingodds$) is shown embedded in the constellation of the Bull. The midpoint of the sign, where the circle meets the crescent in the glyph $\bouncingodds$, is marked by the star Aldebaran at 15° $\bouncingodds$ - which is the exact middle of the sign, since each sign is thirty degrees long. Thus, Aldebaran, marking the Bull's eye at 15° $\bouncingodds$, is at the center of the sign <u>and</u> the constellation of Taurus.

Looking again at the figure on page 19, it can be seen that the star cluster of the Pleiades is located on the upper part of the neck of the constellation of the Bull, and correspondingly on the part of the circle passing through Aldebaran and the Pleiades represented by the circular part of the glyph $\bouncingodds$. In the sidereal zodiac the Pleiades are located at 5° $\bouncingodds$. The two horns of the Bull are marked by the stars Elnath (28° $\bouncingodds$) and Alhecka (30° $\bouncingodds$), which correspond to the tips of the crescent surmounting the sign of Taurus ($\bouncingodds$) – this crescent representing the horns of the Bull.

What is not generally realized is that all twelve signs of the zodiac – represented by their glyphs – originated *directly* from a perception of the flow of spiritual forces within the corresponding constellations.[3] In this sense, the signs truly are embedded in the constellations of the zodiac. Working with the cosmic dances of the signs enables one to enter into the flow of spiritual forces comprising a sign as represented by its glyph, since this provides the basis for the choreography.

In this way a direct experience of the *being* of a zodiacal sign is made possible. This experience is then intensified in moving together with a group of people shaping the cosmic form of that sign. Through the choreography, the group creates the glyph of the sign as a "moving *mandala*" in etheric space, thus attracting the essence of that sign – by way of creating a *resonance* with the sign in the heavens. The creation of this *resonance* with a *cosmic archetype* is a matter of direct experience that grows in profundity in the course of time, so that repeating the cosmic dances enables one to come to ever deeper levels of comprehension of the spiritual nature of the zodiacal signs.

Those who have taken part in the cosmic dances can confirm the deepening knowledge of cosmic archetypes made possible through the dances and also the transforming power of the cosmic dances upon oneself and especially upon the earth at that location. The cosmic dances open up the spiritual kingdom of the earth known as *Shamballa*, the participants weaving together a multi-colored "ethereal flower" in the etheric space at that location. This ethereal flower, magnificently raying out in all directions as a vibrant, enlivening, pulsing *life creation*, is the reality underlying that which is referred to above in a more abstract way as a moving *mandala*.

The Decans
In the contemplation of the constellations as living *beings*, a further defining which describes the *interiority* or inner qualities of each of these vast regions proves to be

---

[3] Robert Powell, *Hermetic Astrology*, vol. I, pages 230–237. See also Robert's works *The Sidereal Zodiac* (co-authored with Peter Treadgold) and *The Zodiac: A Historical Survey*.

helpful. Thus, these materials include descriptions of the subdivisions of the zodiacal signs which are called *decans*. The 36 decans are 10° subdivisions of the zodiac, three decans in each sign.

The decans originated with the Egyptians and are referred to in an ancient text ascribed to the legendary teacher of the Egyptians, Hermes Trismegistus.[4] In this text the *planetary rulers* of the decans are indicated (Saturn ruling the first decan of Pisces, Jupiter ruling the second decan of Pisces, Mars ruling the third decan of Pisces, etc.). The planetary rulerships describe the *quality* or mood of the subdivisions. These planetary rulerships assigned to the decans by Hermes were confirmed as valid by Rudolf Steiner.[5]

The Interchange of Venus and Mercury

These same planetary rulerships are used in the following materials, with the **exception** of the interchange of Mercury and Venus.

Returning to the example of the sign of Taurus: Mercury, the Moon, and Saturn are indicated as the rulers of the three decans of Taurus. For Hermes, and also for Rudolf Steiner, *esoteric Mercury* was *understood* to be the ruler of the first decan of Taurus (having to do with the cosmic unfoldment of planetary evolution).

However, in astronomical science Venus and Mercury are interchanged. This signifies that the planet called *Venus* in astronomical science is considered – from a modern standpoint – as the ruler of the first decan of Taurus. On this account, Mercury and Venus are interchanged throughout the decanal descriptions in this study material, as we seek to discover the relational qualities of the inner work of the decans. Therefore the study materials will refer to these planetary names as they are referred to by *modern astronomy*.[6]

Careful study of the mythology associated with the stars in each decan reveals the accuracy of this interchange. For example, as we have seen, Aldebaran (15° ♉) is at the center of the second Taurus decan ruled by the Moon, and the star cluster of the Pleiades (5° ♉) is located at the center of the first Taurus decan ruled by Venus (*esoteric* Mercury). Since the Pleiades are called the *Seven Sisters*, the rulership (influence) of this Pleiades decan by *Venus* can be felt as an experiential reality (quality of time).

Apart from this detail of the interchange of Venus and Mercury, the planetary rulerships of the decans referred to in the following pages are the same as those indicated by Hermes and confirmed by Rudolf Steiner.

The Greater Body of the Cosmos

As we come into a greater awareness of the cosmic realm as a *relational* field, we can begin to have an understanding of the relationship of the *beings* (constellations) which

---

[4] Wilhelm Gundel, *Neue astrologische Texte des Hermes Trismegistos* ("New Astrological Texts of Hermes Trismegistus").

[5] Rudolf Steiner, *Ancient Myths*, pages 57-58.

[6] Robert Powell, *Hermetic Astrology*, vol. I, pages 103-112, discusses the interchange of Venus and Mercury, and pages 238-261 elaborates upon the decans and their planetary rulers.

inhabit the region which surrounds the zodiacal belt as an expression of the *subtle body* of the zodiac. Just as the human being has a subtle body of life energy which extends beyond the physical form, the images which present themselves as *beings* surrounding the zodiac bring to expression the qualities of the inner work of the decans.

According to traditional astrology each of the 36 decans is associated with one or other of the 36 extra-zodiacal constellations as recorded in Ptolemy's star catalogue in the *Almagest*. The association is given by virtue of the constellation being located above or below the corresponding ten-degree division (decan) of the zodiacal sign.

As the *outer body* of some constellations often comprises such a vast expanse in the heavens, their regions sometimes expand beyond a single decan. In several cases there are shared regions of influence – for example **Auriga** *the Shepherd* extends above the third decan of Taurus and the first decan of Gemini. Likewise, **Orion** *the Hunter* extends below the third decan of Taurus and the first decan of Gemini. Therefore, these two decans are associated with both Auriga and Orion. In the light of cosmic correspondences, however, Auriga is associated primarily with the third decan of Taurus and Orion is associated primarily with the first decan of Gemini, because these are the regions whose cosmic stories most magnify their unique influences.[7]

Modern astronomy has made it possible to more accurately define this *relational* aspect through recording the emanations from the individual stars. These materials include the most recent research findings of Robert Powell concerning the *relationship* of the greater cosmos to the *beings* of the sidereal zodiac. This research reveals the *reality* of the greater cosmos as a *living* productive *working* body of spiritual significance.

Concerning the Meditation Work

In consideration of the cosmos and creation being a *work* in progress, the meditation work has been formulated to give an inner perspective of the spiritual influence of the constellational qualities upon the zodiacal signs. This in turn reveals both the gifts and the challenges inherent in each of the signs. The dates associated with each sign indicate the period of the Sun's passage through the *sidereal* signs of the zodiac, in other words the *reality* of the stars. These dates, which are valid at the present time, may vary by a day or so due to the occurrence of leap years. Quotations from Rudolf Steiner's "Twelve Moods" have been included as an expression of the spiritual quality of the Sun in each sign (see page 115).

---

[7] Robert Powell is planning a thorough writing of these scientific findings concerning the clarification and spiritual significance of the decan system.

Cosmic *Eurythmy*
"In the Image and Likeness…"

Aries – Thinking

Red *"Divine fire of creation"*

C major / A minor

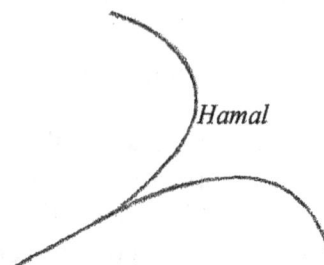

Hamal

The etheric streaming in the group of fixed stars called ***Aries*** provides the cosmic archetypal pattern for the formation of the human head. This flow of divine creative force can be observed in the shaping of the two halves of the human brain which trace the pattern of the two horns of the *Ram*. The etheric streaming connects at the base of the brain and continues down into the formation of the spine and the central nervous system.

Thus, the nervous system of the human being is exquisitely refined and designed to make possible our continued connection with cosmic thought. We are like an inverted "tree of life" with our cosmic roots of etheric life forces generating from heaven.

Correspondingly, it is through our connection to the life currents of the earth, which provide an attracting force, that we are able to maintain our connection with the cosmos. The conjoining of these two forces which *breathe* through us can be experienced as a current of uprightness at one's core.

The eurythmy sound *Vvvv* and the accompanying gestures in the cosmic dance of Aries celebrate this meeting of the *cosmic breath* with the *breath of the earth*.[8] Thus, we bring our appreciation and gratitude to the *body of **Sophia*** of which we are a vital part.

The key of C major is said to represent the *sounding* of Aries. C major bears the clear and clarion sound of resurrection, the promise of new beginnings and the awakening nature of Spring.[9]

Moving to music written in the key of C major, we can experience this bright, sunrise quality. As we touch into the etheric *breath* of the earth with the primal *sound* of Aries – Vvvvv, we can imagine the *dawn* of existence with the *breath* of the divine *breathing* over the face of the earth.

The eurythmy dance form mirrors the etheric streaming of the constellation which is imaged in the glyph for Aries (♈). We see this shape in the human face in the forming of the brows which come together in the center flowing down the line of the nose.

---

[8] In the English language the sound W is a "watery version" of Vvvv. In eurythmy both sounds (W and Vvvv) correspond to Aries.
[9] The relative minor key for Aries is A minor. C major and A minor have the same key signature (no sharps or flats).

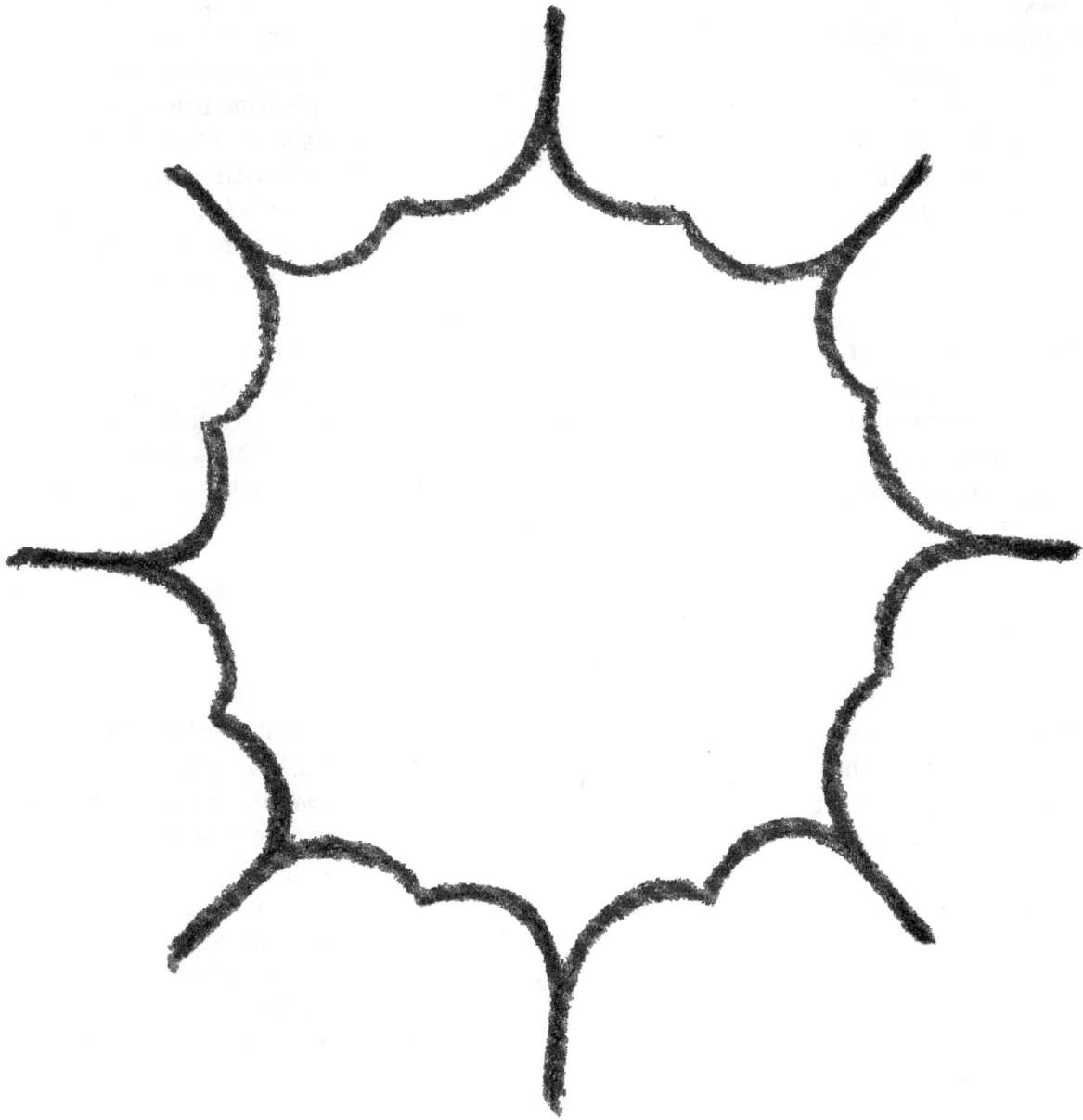

Aries Choreography

Aries Cosmic Dance Form
"The dawn of existence"

Throughout the dance the participants envision the color red, which expresses the mood and quality of the "divine fire of creation".

Aries *Form*:
Beginning with the left foot, make a small curve forward to the left *tracing the first horn of the Ram* and continuing backwards *to the tail of the Ram.*

Backward movement activates the etheric current which streams up the spine opening the crown to receive cosmic thought.

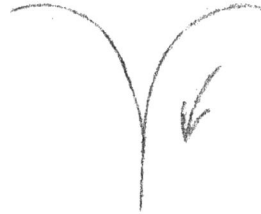

Feeling the current of uprightness

Aries *Gesture*: *While moving back* slowly in a flowing gesture, bring right hand below chin *palm open facing left, fingers extended up toward chin*, completing the gesture as you reach the backward point.

Left arm remains relaxed extending down; palm open facing in toward body, fingers extended *receiving earth forces.*

Vedic *sound Vvvvv*:
Move forward and then curve to the left *forming the arc of the second horn*, while forming the gesture for the sound *Vvvvv.*

Continue by beginning a new ♈ form.

Touching into the breath of the earth ..."and God breathed over the earth".

Sound *Gesture*: *Vvvvv While moving forward and then to the left,* raise arms to heart level. With palms open facing earth, move arms forward in a wavelike motion. *Blessing the earth with cosmic thought.*

Shoulders and head move together following the wavelike flow of the arms and open palms, *inclining toward the earth in a gesture of benediction.*

Repeat Aries *Form*:
Continue curving to the left in an alternating rhythm, stepping forward with left foot (arching to the left) and then moving backwards; then moving forward once again, followed by movement in an arc to left.

Repeat Aries *Gesture/Sound*:
Repeat Aries gesture and sound alternately; forming Aries gesture when moving back and forming the sound Vvvvvv with wavelike movement of arms / hands when moving forward.

The Vedic sound Vvvvvv celebrates the pouring out of God's love for creation

Vvvvvv is a primal sound originating in the early Sanskrit language of the Vedas. We can imagine moving with the first *cosmic breath* of Divine Love, bringing the *divine fire* of creation to the earth.

The eurythmy gesture for Aries activates an etheric streaming which connects the cosmic streaming (*from above*) (flowing into the crown and then down through the spine and central nervous system) with the current which continues up from the earth.

The gesture brings an enlivening force (*through the marriage of these two currents*) to the thymus and thyroid glands bringing them into connection with the pituitary gland (*brow center*) and pineal gland (*within the center of the cranium*).

This brings an experience of the "Hieros Gamos", the sacred marriage of heaven and earth, *spiritualization* and *interiorization*.

Through the movement and gestures of eurythmy, one can come into connection with the regenerative and enlivening forces of the etheric body of Christ which now permeates the etheric realm of the earth.

Thus, the promise initiated through Christ's sacrifice on Golgotha when the Sun was in the middle of the sign of Aries comes to fulfillment.

Aries and "The Bride of the Lamb"
The process of spiritualization (Christ) and interiorization (Sophia)

The Babylonian priest Berossos taught that the "world was created when the Sun was in the *Ram*." In order to further understand this teaching, it is interesting to note that the main star of the constellation of Aries is called ***Hamal***, which in Arabic means "*Lamb*", and in Babylonian the "*Ram's Horn*".

In antiquity the Greeks associated Hamal with ***Athena***, who was born from the head of Zeus, which is in keeping with Berossos' teaching. For when we consider that ***Sophia*** (wisdom) was the first created being and thus the bearer of God's creation (as his reflection), then we have an echo in the story of Athena, who we associate with wisdom and community, revealing herself as a thought of God.

When we consider that Aries is seen in connection with the formation of the human head and the flowing of the central nervous system down into the spine, we can begin to have a sense of the genus of this ancient knowledge.

In star lore Hamal, which marks the eastern horn of the Ram, is also connected with the "legend of the golden fleece" (associated with Christ, the *Lamb of God),* so that here with the two imaginations of Hamal, we have an echo of the "Lamb and his Bride", referring to Christ and Sophia, described by St. John in *The Revelation to John*.

The teachings of Hermes in ancient Egypt contained a pre-Christian understanding of the relationship of the *Lamb and his Bride* through the mystery teachings of ***Isis*** and ***Osiris***.

In these teachings Isis is the primal *gathering* force that continues to bring the *generative* forces of Osiris into wholeness. Osiris was seen in connection with the phases of the Moon. Thus, Isis was recognized and revered as the sustaining force which *re-members* creation.

Through the work of Rudolf Steiner it is known that Moses – and also Hermes, who we associate with the wisdom teachings of ancient Egypt – were pupils of Zarathustra. It was Zarathustra, known to the Greeks as Zoroaster, who brought the wisdom of the stars for the Age of Aries. Moses became the bearer of a very high wisdom in the Age of Aries which culminated with the sacrifice of the "Lamb of God" toward the end of that age.

Moses experienced the *thought of God* with the receiving of the *Ten Commandments* on Mount Sinai during the early part of the Age of Aries. Therefore Moses can be considered one of the great initiates of Aries. Michelangelo, with his powerful sculpture of Moses, depicted the prophet's ability to receive *cosmic thought*. He did so by portraying Moses with two horns coming out of his forehead, an imagination of the two horns of the Ram, symbolizing the 2 petal lotus flower in the region of the brow center, corresponding to Aries and imaged in the glyph ♈.

Aries "*The Ram*" (April 15 – May 15)
The Prince of the Zodiac

The ancient clairvoyants envisaged the body of fixed stars in the constellation of Aries as forming the shape of a Ram. The Ram's head was turned back looking over the body of fixed stars which comprise this region of the heavens. Thus, we have represented in the constellation of stars called Aries, an imagination of the *shepherd* watching over his *flock*.

Legends and myths regarding the images which present themselves in the heavens have existed throughout the ages in all cultures. Therefore, it is not surprising that the starry heavens are said to also bear the stories written in the Gospels regarding the past and future of humanity.

To illustrate this point, we can observe that the *vernal point,* which marks the succession of the zodiacal ages, was actually located in the sign of Aries during the life of Christ, who was referred to as the *Lamb of God* up until about 215 AD, when the vernal point shifted to the constellation of Pisces, the *Fishes*, so that since about 215 AD the *Fish* (Greek: *Ichthys*) has been a symbol for Christ.[10]

Aries is associated with the element of fire. In traditional astrology it is the *home* of the red planet **Mars**. This means that the qualities of Mars, a planet of action also associated with speech, are enhanced by Aries, which astrologers describe as masculine, fiery and cardinal. According to the Egyptian tradition of the decans, Mars is said to have a special rulership over the beginning region of Aries, meaning that the *sound* quality, mood and tone of this early region of Aries is *colored* by Mars, bearing an especially dynamic Martian quality. Here we can imagine, "*In the beginning was the Word…*" the coming of the *Logos* entering into the "*fire* of creation".

Aries is also the place of *exaltation* for the **Sun**, the bestower of life. According to the research of Robert Powell in <u>*Christian Hermetic Astrology,*</u> the region of the exaltation of the Sun in Aries (19° Aries), which is located in the central region of this constellation, was the same region as the location of the Sun during the *transfiguration* (14° Aries) 31 AD, the *crucifixion* (14° Aries) 33 AD and the *resurrection* (15½° Aries) 33 AD of Jesus Christ, referred to in the scriptures as the "*Son* of man." According to the Egyptian system of *decans*, this central region of Aries is *ruled* by the Sun.

Thus, the *heart* (central region) of Aries remembers the Mystery of Golgotha, which was a *Sun Mystery.*

---

[10] The symbol for Christ among the early Christians symbolized the vertical line connecting heaven and earth, and the symbol for Jesus was the cross: I=Christ; X=Jesus; ✶=Jesus Christ. This sign was seen as the symbol of Jesus Christ. This is also the hieroglyph for fish (✶ =fish). The Greek word for fish is IXΘΥΣ – Ichthys (I-Ch-Th-Y-S) which was interpreted as **I**eßoûs **Ch**ristòs **Th**eoû(h) **Y**iòs **S**sotér, which means Jesus Christ, God's Son, Saviour. (Robert Powell, <u>*The Sign of the Son of Man in the Heavens*</u>, p.120).

If we read the starry script that supports this region of the heavens (the central ten degrees of Aries) which is said to be ruled by the Sun, we find yet another amazing correspondence. **Cassiopeia**,[11] "*The Enthroned Woman*" stretches her starry body out as protectress of this region. Known in antiquity as the "queenly woman, matchless in beauty and exalted in dignity", Cassiopeia becomes a symbol for Sophia, "*the woman clothed with the Sun*", described in <u>*The Revelation to John*</u>.

Between Cassiopeia and Aries, the triangle of stars called **Triangulum**, associated with the "*Eye of God*", completes the picture of the beginning of creation.

---

[11] Cassiopeia's main stars create a large "W" in the night sky or an "M" according to one's viewing perspective (location) on the earth.

Aries Meditation Work: *"Devotion becomes force of sacrifice."*

Sun in Aries: April 15 – May 15

It is in the sacrifice of the life of Christ that the Aries virtue of *spiritual strength* finds its archetypal model. Here we have an inherent challenge for the *sovereignty* of the individual not to be sacrificed in the burning *fire* of the *spirit* of devotion, which is generated from the Aries constellation. For it is only through the *self*-confident sovereignty of the individual that true service in the spirit of devotion can be offered.

It is in finding the medium (the middle road) between the two extremes that one develops the Aries *virtue*, which when practiced, leads to the power of self-sacrifice.

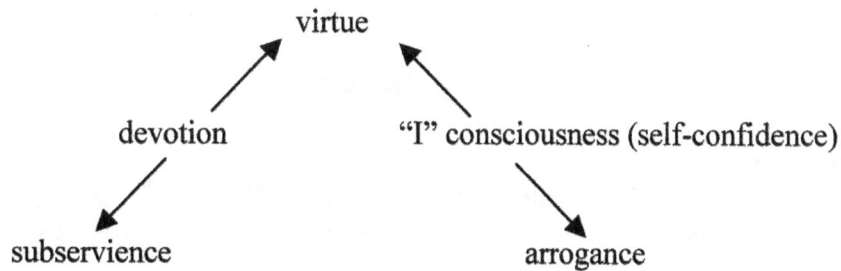

The diagram below can be useful in understanding the inner work and dynamics involved in developing the Aries virtue. The lower two points provide the foundation required to achieve the higher aspect of Aries. The left-hand corner is the virtue. The right-hand corner is what is needed along with the virtue in order to arrive at the uppermost point. The mid-points are what the lower points become if taken to extremes. (For example, devotion taken to an extreme becomes subservience, and self-confidence becomes arrogance. The power of self-sacrifice rests upon devotion and self-confidence.)

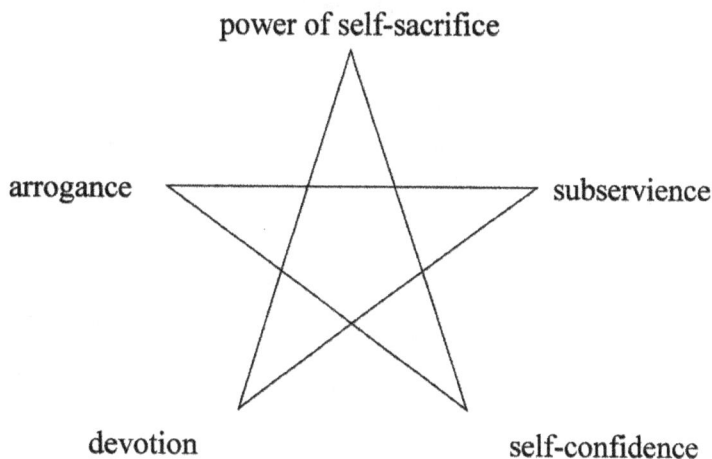

17

Exercise: Control of *thought*
The Archangel St. Michael is very interested in our thinking. When we think a right thought Michael is able to pour in will forces, strengthening the thought.[12]

The Sun Line from the "Twelve Moods"

The first line of each verse of Rudolf Steiner's "Twelve Moods" is the *Sun line* bringing to expression the quality of the Sun in the twelve signs of the zodiac (see page 115). The line for the *Sun in Aries* expresses the quality of *sunrise*:

Sun in **Aries**: *"Arise, O shining light"*

Virtue: Devotion
Sense: For speech (the *living* **word**)
World view: Idealism
Quality: Pioneer; Idealism; "I am" (*strong "I" consciousness*)

Apostle representing Aries: Andrew – the fiery, enthusiastic, first disciple of Jesus.

Historical Examples

Marx, William the Silent, Hitler, Catherine the Great, Kant, Freud, Shakespeare, Novalis – thinkers, philosophers, leaders, demonstrators of the quality (or lack) of *spiritual uprightness*.

Aries – Sun sign (location of the Sun at birth given in degrees in the sidereal zodiac): Charlie Chaplin (4°), Madame de Staël (11°), Turner (11°), Kant (11°), Leonardo da Vinci (16½°), Teilhard de Chardin (18°), Novalis (21°), Marx (21½°), Freud (23½°), Brahms (24°), Tchaikovsky (24°), Shakespeare (24°), Robert Browning (25°), Salvador Dali (27°), Krishnamurti (27½°), Florence Nightingale (29½°).

Aries Political Leaders

first decan – Mars – the Girdle of Andromeda
Thomas Jefferson (2°), Charlemagne (7°), Hitler (7½°), Lenin (9½°).

second decan – Sun – Cassiopeia
The resurrection of Jesus Christ: Sun at 15½° Aries.
William the Silent (15°) – freed Holland from the Spanish occupation.
Czar Alexander II (16°) – freed the serfs in Russia.

third decan – Mercury – the Throne of Cassiopeia
Catherine the Great (20½°) – became Empress of Russia after overthrowing her husband.
Isabella of Castile (23°) – supported Columbus and instigated the inquisition of the Jews.
Robespierre (24°) – beheaded people by having them guillotined (French revolution).
Oliver Cromwell (25°) – overthrew the monarchy in England (executed King Charles I).

---

[12] St. Michael is the Archangel (risen to the level of Time Spirit) in charge of the shepherding of the present Archangelic Age (1879-2233). He is the regent of *cosmic thinking*.

Cosmic *Eurythmy*

"In the Image and Likeness..."

Taurus – Will

Orange *"Inner warmth reveals essence"*

G major / E minor

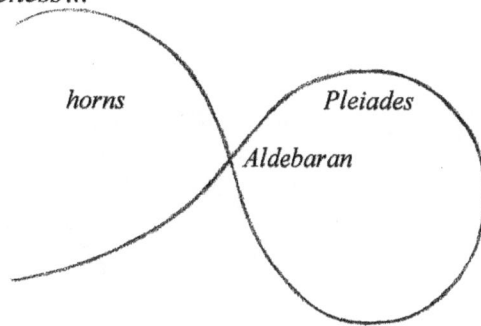

horns

Pleiades

Aldebaran

The refinement of the human head continued over many thousands of years until the shaping of the larynx and eustachian tubes made possible the faculty of speech and spiritual hearing. The shaping force for the formation of the organs of speech generate from the region of the heavens which is known as **Taurus**, the *Bull.*

In this realm *thought* becomes **word**. The alchemy of the *turning* of the fiery nature of cosmic thought brings about a *warming* of the heart forces. (We see this *turning* in the *spiraling* pattern of horns which bring cosmic forces into the rounding of the head.) A metamorphosis takes place, wherein the spoken word becomes the bearer of moral substance. Clarity of thought becomes the generating force for the human will.

Now, the harmony of the heart and the head bring a *warmth* to the clarity of the fiery red of cosmic *thought* (**Aries**). We imagine ourselves immersed in the warming glow of the color orange, a *warming* which reveals to us our *inner essence*, as we move this form to music written in the key of G major, which we associate with the cosmic *sounding* of **Taurus**. With the key of G major we can experience the tempering warmth of sound progressing from the beginning initiatory sound of C major in Aries.

In the movement form, which traces the pattern of the astrological sign for Taurus (♉), we are brought into an immediate experience of the taking in of the full *round* of experience on Earth, drawing this up into the warming crucible of heart and head, and then the out-streaming of the spiritualized will forces as we move forward into the world with the cosmic sounding of Taurus, *Rrrrrr.*

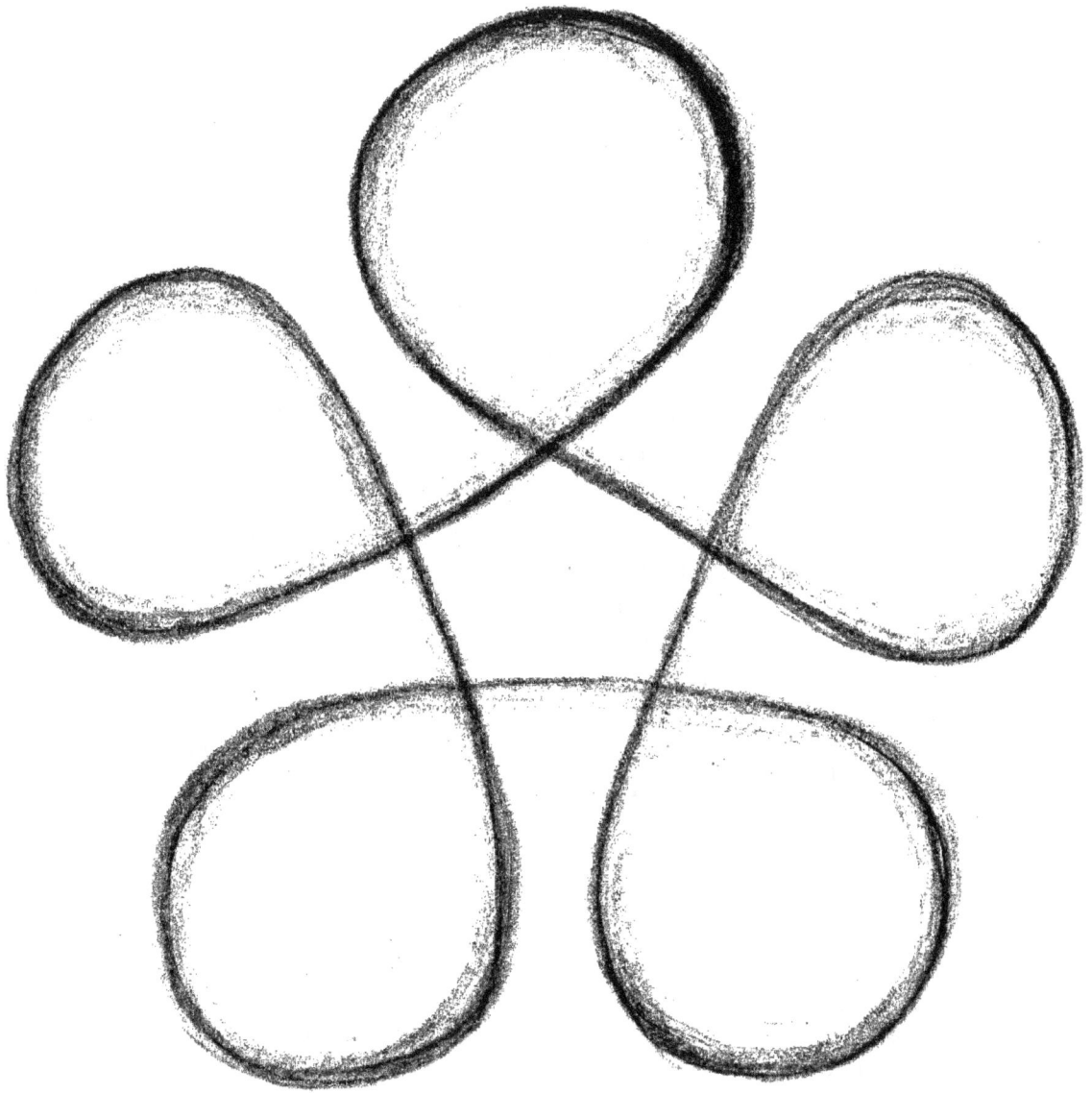

Taurus Choreography

Taurus Cosmic Dance Form
"Thy will be done..."

Taurus *Form*:
Moving to the left and back around to the right,

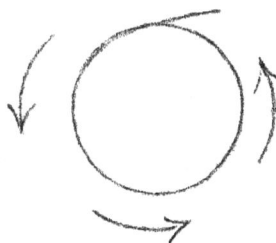

Note: *This circling to the left corresponds to the flowing of etheric forces in the movements of the planets around the zodiac.*

Movement to the left *opens us to receive...*

Movement back *activates the streaming up of etheric life, which moves up through the spine and opens the crown to receive cosmic thought.*

Movement to the right *activates the giving/ sending, active streaming within us (the will).*

Movement forward *brings cosmic thought down through the crown toward the earth.*

Thus with our stepping in a circle in this way, we balance and activate the life force of our etheric body, *coming into alignment with the Cosmic Christ. "Thy will be done on earth as it is in heaven".*

"Self Assertion"

"Activating the will"

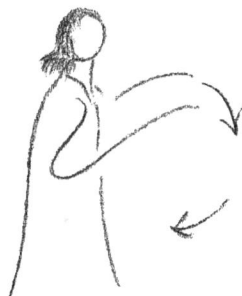

Taurus *Gesture*:
Form the Taurus gesture *while circling back to the left,* completing the gesture at the midpoint of the back of the circle.

Slowly, in a flowing gesture, bring the left hand with closed fist *lightly clenched* in front of the throat. *Head erect and pulled back into alignment with spine, opening the throat center.*

Simultaneously, raise the right arm to encircle the head, palm open extending down towards left ear.

The throat becomes the mediating "listening" center between heart and head.

Taurus *sound*: *Rrrrrr*
While moving forward, arms are rotating back/up, then out/forward, down and around, palms open facing earth.

With the Rrrrrr sound we draw the breath of the earth up into the heart to be transformed by cosmic thought. Then we move cosmic thought out into willed activity blessing the earth.

Repeat Taurus *form*:
Continue circling to the left, moving back to the left, circling around to the right, completing the circle by curving forward to the left.

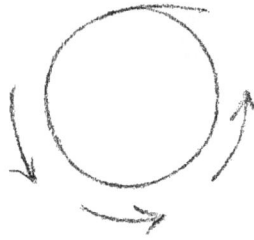

Repeat Taurus *gesture/ sound*: *alternately forming Taurus gesture while moving back and around and then forming the sound Rrrr when moving forward.*

The *wisdom* of cosmic will is inherent in the movement of the sound *Rrrrrr*.

With palms perpendicular to the arm, we are open to receive the forces which flow into the heart. *In this way we take in the breath of the earth.*

With palms extended straight in alignment with the arms, we actively send out currents of life energy, *flowing from the will of the heart blessing the earth.*

The Taurus gesture is made possible through the gift of our uprightness which creates a space for the cosmic forces received through the crown to gather in the throat.

With the Taurus gesture, the throat center (larynx and thyroid gland) becomes the mediating center between heart and head.

The gesture activates a circulation pattern which flows (from the heart center) counterclockwise up and over the head. The open right palm sends a warming radiation throughout the cranium. The gesture directs the flowing of etheric currents from the crown which bring stimulation to the eustachian tubes (spiritual listening center).

With the closed left hand held in front of the throat center, the streaming of life currents from the heart are concentrated and radiating into the throat center.

The activity of *moral* speaking is enhanced through the streaming of life currents between the heart center and the crown. This circulation creates a concentrated center (throat) of heightened sense ability to serve as a receiver (eustachian tubes) for the activity of spiritual listening.

"The Royal Way"
The path of initiation

The impulse of Taurus works toward the transformation of one's lower astral nature bringing forward the higher aspect of the human being, the "Holy Animality" nature *(Meditations on the Tarot, Arcanum X)* in which the **Bull** represents divine will.

Thus, with Taurus we begin our connection with the "Royal Way", the higher path of Christ and *initiation*, entailing the work of transformation indicated by the naming of the "Four Holy Living Creatures" by St. John in *The Revelation to John*: the Bull, the Lion, the Eagle, and the Man or Angel.

The ancient Persian astrologers recognized **Aldebaran** (15°Taurus) marking the "eye of the *Bull*" as one of the "Four Royal Stars" which define the directional axis of heaven: Aldebaran in the East together with Antares (15°Scorpio) in the West, Regulus (5°Leo) in the North and Fomalhaut (9°Aquarius) in the South. These four stars form a cross in the heavens marking the four directions of space. The *"Four Royal Stars"* bear a rich lineage, for it was the great Persian teacher Zarathustra who first designated their *royalty*, calling them the "Four Guardians of Heaven" or the "Watchers in the Four Directions," with Aldebaran, as the *"Watcher in the East"*,[13] also called the *"Eye of God"*.

According to the research of Robert Powell in *Christian Hermetic Astrology*, the *transfiguration* of Jesus Christ took place when the Moon's ascending node[14] (gateway to the astral world) was in conjunction with Aldebaran, the "Eye of God."

Thus, the starry script which marked the time of the *transfiguration* provides a beautiful archetypal image for the working impulse of Taurus. The **Moon**, which finds her place of *exaltation* in Taurus, remembers the karma of our lower nature. With the conjunction of the Moon's ascending node with Aldebaran, we have a coming together of the Moon's gateway opening to the Sun and – beyond the Sun – to the stellar "Eye of God."

Some esotericists speak of the **Pleiades** in the region of the neck of the Bull (5°Taurus) as marking the "hub of our galaxy". The cluster of stars called the *Pleiades* is associated with the myth of the *Seven Daughters of Atlas*, who wept for their father's toil in shouldering the world, and were rewarded for their compassion by becoming stars. Thus, the Pleiades are sometimes referred to as *"The Seven Sisters"*.

The 19th century German astronomer Johann Heinrich von Mädler calculated that our galaxy is revolving around **Alcyone** , the main star in the Pleiadian cluster, and according to Rudolf Steiner the progress of Earth evolution is headed toward the cosmic *outbreathing* of the Pleiades, moving us toward the "Word of God".[15]

---

[13] Around 3000 BC Aldebaran marked the position of the vernal point on the first day of Spring when the Sun rose in the East on the day of the Spring Equinox.

[14] Moon's Nodes mark the points of intersection of the path of the Moon with the apparent path of the Sun.

[15] Perhaps on this account the Babylonians recognized that the Moon finds its place of exaltation in the region of the Pleiades. The Pleiades are mentioned in the Book of Job in the praising of the Creator, "Who made the Bear and Orion, the Pleiades and the chambers of the south" (*Job* 9:9). Job was the great-great-grandfather of Abraham. (Footnote 15 continued on next page.)

When we ponder the images presented by the myths and legends of the starry constellation of Taurus, we can begin to understand Taurus as a vessel (*interiorization*) for the Divine fire (*spiritualization*) initiated in Aries. The great work of transformation has begun.

The Heavenly Body of Cosmic Life Forces

The research of Robert Powell has revealed the star **Rigel** 22° Taurus, the star marking the western foot of **Orion**, whose luminosity is estimated to be 42,000 times greater than our Sun, to be the *star of the ascension*, as the Sun was in conjunction with this star during the *ascension* of Jesus Christ.

Here the word "conjunction", has to be understood in an expanded sense, since **Rigel,** although its longitude in the sidereal zodiac is 22° Taurus (♉), is located 31 degrees south of the ecliptic which passes through the center of the belt of the zodiac.

The great circle or "meridian" passing from the north to the south pole of the ecliptic and running through Rigel intersects the ecliptic/zodiac at 22° ♉ . Just as every point on a meridian (line of energy flow) in the human being is connected to every other point on the meridian line (through the flow of energy along the meridian), so every star on the "Rigel meridian" running through 22° ♉ is connected with Rigel. Therefore when the Sun, Moon, or any planet, is at 22° ♉ , it is "in conjunction" with Rigel via the Rigel meridian.

The actual location of the Sun at the *ascension* was 23° ♉ [16], just one degree from the Rigel meridian, and hence in conjunction with Rigel (in this expanded sense of the word "conjunction").

By implication, every star in the heavens is important, acting along its meridian, indicated by the zodiacal degree of the intersection of that meridian with the ecliptic. The greater the star's luminosity, the more significant it is in terms of its spiritual influence. Thus, Rigel, which is one of 30 *megastars* in our cosmos with a luminosity more than 10,000 times greater than our Sun, is a highly significant star of extraordinary spiritual intensity.

(Footnote 15 continued from previous page.) The Maori people of New Zealand start the New Year with the heliacal rising of the Pleiades, or rather with the first New Moon after the appearance (heliacal rising) of the Pleiades in June. The Pleiades are called "Matariki" by the Maori, who say at the start of the New Year: "Divine Matariki, come hither from the distant heavens; bestow the first fruits of the year upon us."
[16] See *Chronicle of the Living Christ,* p. 177.

Taurus "The Bull" (May 15 – June 16)

Taurus is the divine archetype which shapes our throat and activates our throat chakra. In the shaping of our larynx and eustachian tubes we see a mirroring of the stethoscope used in medicine. Just as the medical doctor listens to the sound of the heart, so too we are designed in wisdom to listen to the heart of God, via the instrument of our "inner stethoscope", corresponding spiritually to the larynx and the eustachian tubes. The throat chakra then activates our center for *spiritual listening*.

The age of Taurus (when the *vernal point* resided in the constellation of Taurus) marked the zenith of the ancient Egyptian culture. The Egyptians were a *listening* culture related to the sense of inspiration. Their religious practices and customs brought a studied awareness of the generating forces of the starry heavens upon the responsive activity of the forces in nature. Certain bright stars rising in the East or setting in the West were considered kings, and the Egyptian temples of initiation, the pyramids and sphinx were all built with a calculated orientation. Some were oriented toward the rising and the setting of the stars; the star "Sirius" and the three stars in the "Belt of Orion" were especially important. Others were oriented toward the four main solar phenomena of the year – the summer and winter solstices, when the Sun appears to come to a stop, and the spring and autumn equinoxes, when the night and day are of equal length.

We recognize the pattern of the sign of Taurus in the image and iconography of *Isis* depicted with the Moon above her head, and also in the image of the *sacred Cow* with the guiding star Sirius above, between the Cow's horns.

The revered Goddess *Nut* stretches *her* (Sophianic) starry body in a protective gesture over the arched surfaces of the interiors of the burial tombs of the Egyptian Pharaohs and Queens. Thus, the Egyptian tombs reveal a *faith* in the possibility of the resurrection body which was fulfilled by the *ascension* of Jesus Christ, when the Sun stood at 23° ♉ Taurus.[17] We see this mirrored in the astrological sign for Taurus with the upturned *arc* above the circle, an imagination of the Moon "*gathered*" into fullness (becoming a *Sun*) beneath the "*Grail Moon*", the New Moon's promise of *resurrection*.

The Starry Script
To complete this lunar imagination, we find that the starry script which supports the *etheric body* of Taurus tells the story of the work of the soul.[18] For the stars which form the body of the great *cosmic river Eridanus* add their etheric flow to the central region of Taurus, which is said to be *ruled* by the Moon (in the Egyptian system of the decans).

 We associate the Moon with the forces that move waters and also the Moon bears the memory of our soul karma which is presented to us in the ebb and flow of our daily lives, symbolized by *Eridanus*, the mover of life which flows from the *source* to the *future*.

---

[17] Robert Powell, *Chronicle of the Living Christ*, p. 177.
[18] This is the starry script imaged in the heavens in the constellations above and below the constellation of Taurus, related to the three decans of Taurus (Perseus relating to the 1st decan, Eridanus to the 2nd decan, and Auriga to the 3rd decan.)

During the two and one half days each month when the Moon transits Taurus, the Moon's intensity is increased, which affects the human being's receptivity to astral influences.

The planet **Venus** also has a special relationship to Taurus, *ruling* over the entire constellation. She is especially strong in the beginning region of Taurus where the Pleiades (5° ♉), which are called the "Seven Sisters", are located. Here the starry body of the hero *Perseus* brings his etheric force to rescue the fair *Andromeda*. Andromeda represents the divine feminine or the *soul* of humanity.

According to legend *Athena* (wisdom) serves as guide for *Perseus* to overcome the astrality of the *atavistic* feminine nature by cutting off the head of *Medusa*, marked by the star *Algol* (1½° ♉), which is known as the "eye of the Medusa".

Thus, **Perseus** stands behind this region of the first decan of **Taurus** as a guardian for the astral forces which are stirred by the receptivity of the Moon's influence over the region. The Moon finds its place of *exaltation* in the region of the *Pleiades* (5° ♉).[19]

And, finally, **Auriga** (the Shepherd) brings his starry nature to *shepherd* the completion (third decan) of Taurus. We recognize *Auriga*, holding the *she* goat and watching over two little goat kids. We recall that the Sun stood in this final region of Taurus during the *ascension* of Jesus Christ (Sun at 23°Taurus). *"He shall gather the lambs with his arm and carry them in his bosom, and shall gently lead those that suck" (Isaiah 40:10-11).* Thus with the *rising* of *Auriga*, we can remember Christ's *ascension* to the Father.

If we gather the images presented in the legends and myths associated with the constellation of Taurus, we can begin to feel the feminine nature of Taurus, the caring for beauty, the human soul and nature. Taurus is considered an Earth sign, with a special caring for earthly life and the material world.

To summarize, the **three decans of Taurus** are:

first decan – Venus – Perseus

second decan – Moon – Eridanus (the River)

third decan – Saturn – Auriga (the Shepherd, also called the Charioteer)

---

[19] A Babylonian cuneiform text depicted the Moon exalted in the Pleiades. In listing the zodiacal degree of the Moon's exaltation as 3° ♉ the question is whether actually 5° ♉ is meant, which is the longitude of the Pleiades.

Taurus Meditation Work: *"Inner balance becomes progress."*

Sun in Taurus: 15 May – 16 June

Taurus is a feminine sign, with a deep connection to the earth. Taurus is *ruled* by Venus whose qualities are especially strong in the first decan (10°). The place of *exaltation* for the forces of the Moon, the planet closest to the earth, is in the region of the star cluster of the Pleiades at 5°Taurus.

As the *vessel* for Aries, Taurus is considered an Earth sign, concerned with the bringing down of cosmic thought into daily existence.

The work of the transformation of the Will: *"May the world thought think in me."*

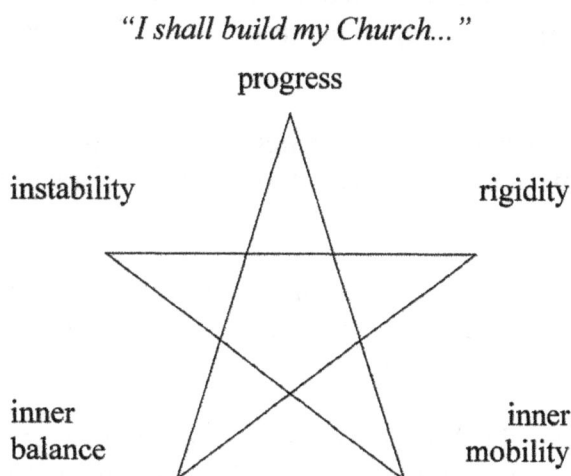

"I shall build my Church..."

progress

instability   rigidity

inner
balance   inner
mobility

The lower two points provide the foundation required to achieve the higher aspect of Taurus. The lower left hand corner is the virtue. The lower right hand corner is what is needed along with the virtue in order to arrive at the uppermost point. The mid-points are what the lower points become if taken to extremes.

Virtue:	Inner balance
Sense:	Thought
World view:	Rationalism
Exercise:	Control of *will*

Sun in **Taurus:** *"Become bright radiant being."*

The Earth sign of Taurus has given birth to many of the great poets, orators and writers rendering the gift of language which bears moral substance.

The writer Balzac, born under the sign of Taurus (Sun at 7½°), was known for his strong will and constitution, with a brilliant descriptive ability. (Taureans take in the world around them.) It is said that he drank at least 30 cups of coffee a day. Coffee stimulates the adrenals which are governed by the spleen (the Earth organ).

The American poet Walt Whitman (Sun at 17°) wrote with descriptive force of the wonders of nature. Thomas Mann (22°), Thomas Hardy (19°), W.B. Yeats (30°), Arthur Conan Doyle (8°), John F. Kennedy (14°) all sought each in their own way to bring moral substance to the *living* word.

Historical examples of Sun in **Taurus**

St. Luke is the archetypal representative amongst the four evangelists that represents Taurus. He was a scribe and physician.

Richard Wagner (May 22), the great German poet and composer was born when the Sun (8½°) was in the neck of the Bull (spiritual listening), which served as substance for the music and texts of his seven major operas describing the path of *initiation*.[20] Wagner wrote the words to his own operas as well as composing them. The composer Schumann was also inspired by Taurus (June 10); in his case the Sun (25°) was in the region of the horns of the Bull.

Among the disciples, the archetypal figure representing Taurus is Peter, known as the "Foundation Stone", to whom Jesus spoke, *"Thou art the rock upon which I shall build my church"*.

Following the *"build my church"* impulse, Emperor Charles IV (Sun at 15½°), the great Bohemian Emperor, built Karlstein (*Grail Castle*) near Prague, to whom Rudolf Steiner referred as the last great *initiate* Emperor.

Metternich was an influential politician who worked toward increasing the power of the Austrian Empire. The Sun at his birth was at 3°, close to the Pleiades at 5°.

Machiavelli (Sun at 4½°) demonstrated the will to power of the *lower self*, while Fichte (Sun at 7°) brought the philosophy of the "I", the *willing* of the *higher self*. John Paul II, the Polish pope (3½°), models the force of the transformed *will* – as well as Padre Pio (Sun at 11°), the twentieth century Italian saint, whose words bore the substance of the stigmata and changed human lives. (Towards the end of his life some one million people a year came to experience his daily celebration of the Mass.)

Concerning the human will, Mesmer (Sun at 11°) pioneered hypnotism as a therapy. (Of course, this could be an example of one's own will subordinating another's will.)

Other significant **Taurus** Individuals

Philosopher Bertrand Russell (5°), Queen Victoria of England (10°), American author and transcendentalist Emerson (11½°), dancer Isadora Duncan (13°), King Philip II of Spain (21°), painter Albrecht Dürer (21°), painter Gauguin (24°), and composer Richard Strauss (27½°).

---

[20] Robert Powell, *Hermetic Astrology*, vol. II explores this theme further.

Cosmic *Eurythmy*
"In the Image and Likeness..."

Gemini – Capability

Ⅱ Yellow – *"Clarity of thought"*

D major / B minor

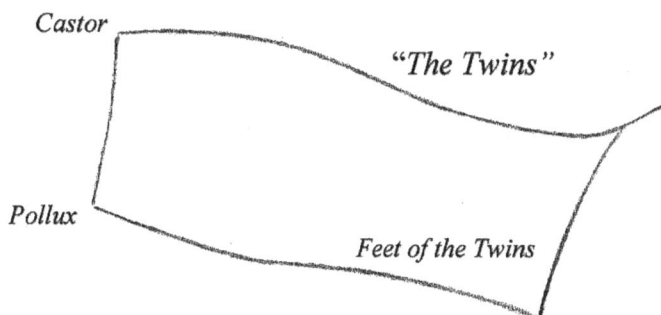

Castor

"*The Twins*"

Pollux

Feet of the Twins

The stars which gather in the constellation of Gemini bear the formative force for the human collar bone, sometimes referred to as the *yoke* or *mantle* of the human being. "*My yoke is easy, and my burden is light*" (*Matthew* 11:30). These words describe the shoulder girdle which connects our two arms and the connecting energy which flows between our hands. We are reminded of this connection in the forming of the astrological sign for Gemini (Ⅱ).

The human collar bone is an instrument of sound, sensitive and attuned to music, rendered through a *feeling* for sound. Thus, Gemini brings an attunement to cosmic thought through our *feeling* nature. Just as our arms are said to be the wings of the heart, correspondingly our arms and hands are capable of expressing profound levels of feeling. *We see this beautifully expressed in Raphael's paintings of the Madonna and in Michelangelo's sculpture of the Pieta.*

We see in the astrological sign for Gemini (Ⅱ), *The Twins,* the ideal of partnership, relationship, and brotherhood, which is the foundation for the building of community. The work of Gemini is the marriage of intellect and heart, the building of true community through the union of wisdom and love.

People born under this sign are very often capable doers with their arms and hands. Gemini renders the ability for action – bringing a sense for dexterity, as well as a highly attuned intellectual grasp and ability to cope with the daily endeavors of life.

We experience the capable, *doing* nature inspired in Gemini in the forming of the eurythmy gesture of Gemini with arms folded confidently across the chest, as well as the outburst of *feeling* life which streams from the heart into the arms and hands with the eurythmy sound "Ha", which may be described as "*joyfully opening to the world*".

In the spirit of the Sun which marries the intellect with the heart, we imagine ourselves surrounded in the radiance of the sun-like color yellow, as we move to music written in the key of D major or the key of B minor.

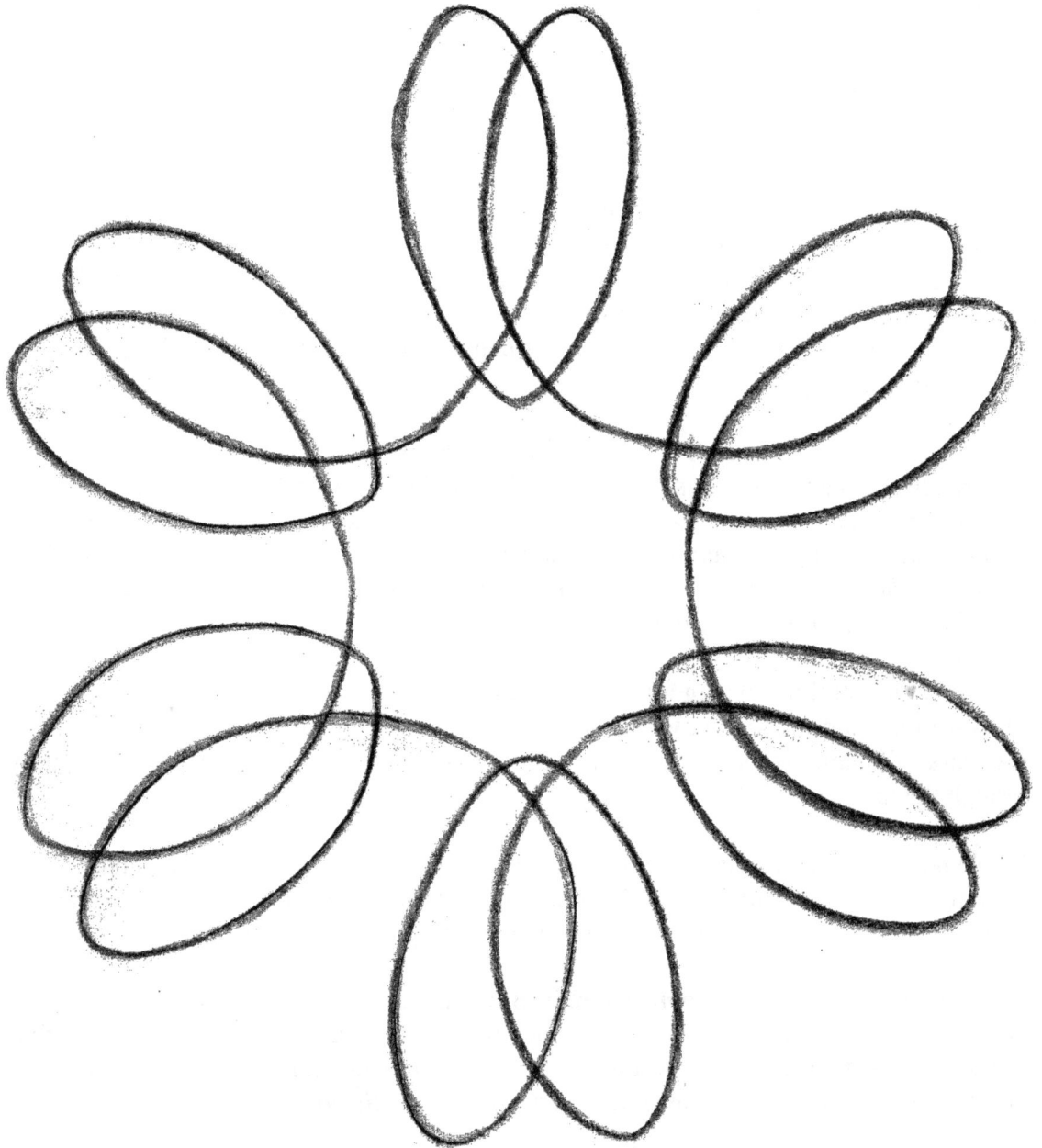

Gemini Choreography

Gemini Cosmic Dance Form
"Joyfully opening to the world"

Gemini *Eurythmy* Form: *Cosmic thought > Cosmic will > Action*
The Gemini form combines the movement of Aries (*Thinking*) and Taurus (*Willing*).

Gemini is an air sign associated with the functioning of the human being's lung organs. We can see the formation of the two lungs in the pattern of the Gemini form.

Gemini *Form*:
Elongated loops back and to the left. Begin by moving back to the left and making a small curve to the right.

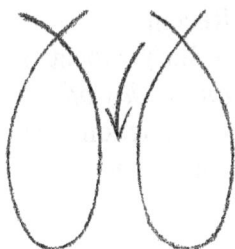

Gemini *Gesture*: *While moving back* fold arms across chest *closed fists resting against inside surface of arms*, completing the gesture at the <u>back</u> of the loop.

This gesture brings the head into alignment with the spine, creating a strong ground for the balance of left/right which is concentrated in the heart center through the closing of the palms.

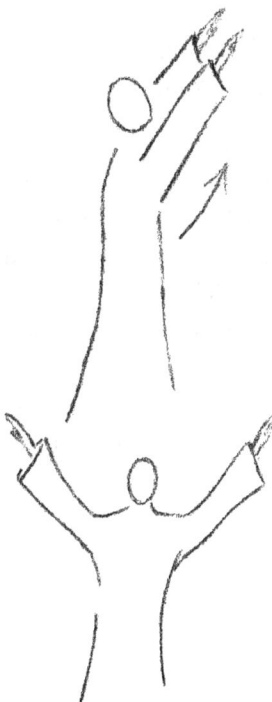

Move forward, curving around to the left *while forming the sound "Ha"*.

Gemini Sound: "Ha"
While moving forward arms and hands *burst* open and *joyfully* flow up and widen, completing the gesture at the <u>front</u> of the loop.

"The sound "Ha" streams from the feeling heart into the arms/hands."

Continue Form: Continue moving, *forming elongated loops*, curving back to the left and moving forward to complete the loop.

Alternately forming the Gemini gesture with *arms folded* across chest while moving back, and forming the eurythmy sound "Ha" *while moving forward*.

For the experience of partnership experiment with moving in pairs

Gemini *"The Twins"* (June 16 – July 17)
"....the two shall become one."

The fixed stars in the region of Gemini, which means twinship, were seen by the ancient clairvoyants as two young men walking arm in arm, exuding a feeling of brotherhood. In our time (due to the precession of the vernal point), the Sun, the heart of our solar system, is in the *Twins*[21] when it is nearing its zenith point at the time of the Summer Solstice.

Thus, we associate Gemini with the warmth and energizing forces of the Sun. Gemini brings an attunement to the feeling heart of God, the flames of Divine Love pulsing from the *Great Central Sun.*

The Heart of God
Our Milky Way galaxy intersects the fixed band of zodiacal stars in the region of the feet of the Twins (first few degrees of Gemini). According to recent scientific findings regarding the dating of events in the life of Christ, we learn that 2°Gemini (within this band of intersection) marked the Sun's location on the day of *Pentecost,* when the disciples experienced tongues of fire pulsing from the heart of God.[22] Recent astronomical findings have discovered that the *Galactic Center* (Central Sun) is located at 2°Sagittarius, *which is directly opposite the Sun's location (2°Gemini) on the day of Pentecost.* If viewed from the Sun, the Earth would have been seen in conjunction with the Galactic Center. Thus, through the flames of Divine Love the disciples could understand and speak in tongues and in all languages.

John the Beloved, the disciple whom Jesus loved, is the archetypal image of the Gemini individuality, attuning to the Heart of God. The Gospels describe him at the Last Supper with his head resting on the breast of Jesus listening to the rhythm of Christ's heart, which connects us to our cosmic brotherhood.

Brotherhood – the Two Becoming One
The archetypal story of brotherhood is found in the stories of the two Jesus children described in the biblical accounts recorded in the books of Saint Luke and Saint Matthew. The birth of Jesus recounted in the Gospel of Saint Luke describes the birth of the *Nathan* Jesus, the *love* child born in a cave (*within*) and visited by shepherds.[23] The *Nathan* Jesus was *born from the "pure" stream, having never been incarnated before, and thus not affected by the Fall.* The Gospel of Saint Matthew describes the birth of the *wise* child who was visited by the three kings, the magi, who were guided by the Star of Zarathustra[24]. This was the *Solomon* child from the line of King David, having descended from David's son Solomon. The *Solomon* child at age seventeen passed over (*spiritually*) into Jesus of Nazareth when Jesus was twelve years old – teaching the elders in the Temple. Christ is the Sun which united the two souls. *"And he was wise beyond his years..."*

---

[21] Castor (25½° ♊) and Pollux (28½° ♊), which mark the heads of the Twins, are the two main stars.
[22] The Heart of God – 2°Sagittarius marks the location of the Galactic Center, the great Central Sun of our galaxy – exactly opposite 2°Gemini, where the Sun was at Pentecost.
[23] This child is called the Nathan Jesus, having descended from King David via David's son Nathan.
[24] Robert Powell, <u>Chronicle of the Living Christ</u> for a more complete description of the Nathan Jesus (described in the Gospel of St. Luke) and the Solomon Jesus (described in the Gospel of St. Matthew).

Solomon Jesus – *Radiant Star*

The great teacher of the ancient Persian culture, Zarathustra, reincarnated in the sixth century BC as Zoroaster, who taught the Babylonian priesthood to await the "star" which would mark his return to Earth, as the Solomon Jesus. This is the mystery of the "Star of the Magi", which was a guiding light for the great astronomer and mathematician, Johannes Kepler.

19° Gemini marks the location of *Sirius*, which is said to be the star of the Solomon Jesus.[25] Sirius was called the *King of Kings* and was revered by the Egyptians as "*Her Majesty, the star of Isis*", the pre-Christian manifestation of Sophia in her cosmic-spiritual form.

Sirius (19° ♊) marks the mouth of *Canis Major*, the *Greater Dog*, also called the "*Prince*".[26] Sirius has a luminosity 24 times brighter than our Sun and moves with a smaller companion which has approximately the same mass as our Sun but is also almost 50 times smaller and is thus known as a White Dwarf. Said to be the star of 1,000 colors, Sirius is certainly the most *radiant star* in our heavens, reaching its culmination in mid-February each year.[27]

The Mystery of the Two Becoming One

With Gemini we begin the great work contained in the mystery of the "two becoming one." One's individual task is to overcome the forces of duality in order to connect with one's higher self. The work is to marry the forces of one's lower nature with the higher intentions of divine will which come to expression through the "I", the higher self or divine nature of the individuality.

Thus, we can experience how the great work begun in Taurus in the training of the will is expressed in Gemini through action, wherein love and truth become the ability to *shoulder* responsibility through the activity of caring for the "other".

This mystery of the "two becoming one" comes to expression archetypally in the esoteric understanding of the divine mystery of John the Baptist who became one with Lazarus, in the raising of Lazarus from the dead. This is an example of a *twinship* with the purpose to *serve*, which was foretold with the birth of John the Baptist when the Sun was in the sign of Gemini, the *Twins*.[28]

Likewise, there is the story of the two Marys, whose *twinship* served as vessel to nurture the divine child who would become the ultimate bearer of the Christ, which occurred at the Baptism in the Jordan.

---

[25] Johanna Keyserlingk, *The Birth of a New Agriculture*, p. 89: "Rudolf Steiner said, 'Sirius is the heart of Jesus-Zarathustra'…"

[26] "Unto us a son is given and the government shall be on his *shoulder* and his name shall be *Prince of Peace*" (*Isaiah* 9:67).

[27] 16° ♊ marks the conception of Solomon Jesus and 14° ♊ marks his death. The Solomon Jesus was called "radiant star". The Egyptian Dendera Zodiac named the Sirius region "Apes" meaning head or leader.

[28] Robert Powell, *Chronicle of the Living Christ*, Appendix V.

Later Mary became a vessel for the divine *Sophia*, making possible the pouring in of the Holy Spirit, described as "tongues of flames" on the heads of the twelve disciples.[29] This holy *twinship* occurred at Pentecost when the Sun stood at 2° Gemini directly opposite the galactic center, the great Central Sun of our galaxy, the fiery center of the heart of God.[30]

Wisdom – Guiding Lights in the Region of Gemini

Mercury, the planet of reason and intelligence is especially at *home* in Gemini. As the "*messenger of the Gods*" the planet Mercury is nearest the Sun. Legend associates Mercury with *Hermes*, the fleet-footed winged messenger of the gods, who – viewed heliocentrically – orbits the entire zodiac in less than three months. Hermes lends a lively quality to the masculine nature of Gemini which is associated with the element of Air.

Orion, the great cosmic hunter brings his cosmic force to the beginning region of Gemini, the *decan ruled by Jupiter*, the planet we associate with *wisdom*. We feel this influence strongly with the three stars in *Orion's belt* which are called the *Three Kings*, referring to the three magi who brought the wisdom of the past epochs of time to the child Jesus.[31] "*Righteousness shall be the girdle of his waist*" (*Isaiah* 11:5).

With **Sirius**, the *star of Isis*, the "radiant star" in the constellation of **Canis Major**, we have yet another influence of wisdom. **Sirius** (19° ♊) marks the mouth of the *Greater Dog*, in this region of Gemini which is *ruled by Mars,* the planet which governs *speech*.

The star **Procyon**, the "*Redeemed Redeemer*" in **Canis Minor,** the *Lesser Dog,* follows **Sirius**, the "*King of Kings*" (19° ♊) and also **Canopus** (20° ♊), the *star of Osiris*, marking the oar of **Argo,** the great *ship of redemption*. Canopus thus adds its guiding light to the Twins. **Canopus** was called the "*star of Egypt*" and in Persian "Suhail", which means *wisdom*.

The guiding lights of **Sirius**, the *King of Kings*, **Procyon**, the *Redeemed Redeemer,* and **Canopus**, the *star of Egypt,* bring quite an impressive line of support for the great intentions of Gemini. Through the influence of **Mercury**, known as the "*Great Cosmic Educator*", there is a strong teaching quality manifesting from the constellation of Gemini, which is in the spirit of co-operation.

---

[29] *Chronicle of the Living Christ* describes the esoteric background to this event and also contains three archetypal accounts of the "two becoming one": two Jesuses, two Marys, and two Johns.

[30] Ideal: "*Where two or more are together, there am I in the midst of them*" (*Matthew* 18:20). The antithesis of Brotherhood – Saturn at 4° ♊ marked the beginning of WWI and also D-Day toward the end of WWII. During the second Gulf War (2003), heliocentric Saturn was approaching 4° ♊ in conjunction with Betelgeuze (see footnote 31).

[31] The three stars in Orion's belt, associated with the three kings, point directly to Sirius, the star of the Master Jesus, to whom the three Magi paid homage. Sirius (19° ♊) is in the central decan of Gemini, and Betelgeuze, the bright star of Orion's right shoulder, is in the first decan of Gemini (4° ♊). The stars of Orion span primarily the first decan of Gemini and the third decan of Taurus, with the three stars in Orion's belt being located in the last part of the third Taurus decan (27½° – 30° ♉).

Gemini Meditation work: *"Perseverance becomes faithfulness..."*

Sun in Gemini: 16 June – 17 July

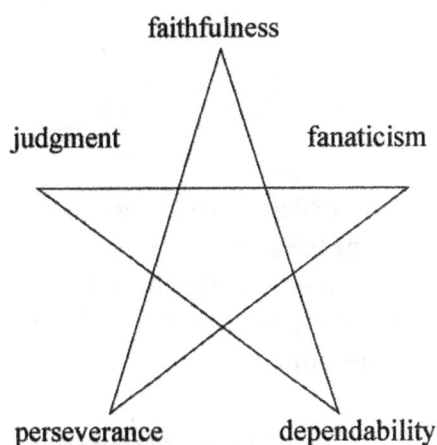

faithfulness

judgment   fanaticism

perseverance   dependability

There is a spirit of morality within each one of us. However, with each life we are tested anew. Gemini brings the faculty of *judgment*.

The Gemini influence can bring a sense of duality, duplicity, a certain fickleness of spirit.

The task is through the mediating *wisdom* of the *heart* to persevere and "fight the *good fight*."

The lower two points provide the foundation required to achieve the higher aspect of Gemini. The lower left-hand corner is the virtue. The lower right-hand corner is what is needed along with the virtue in order to arrive at the uppermost point. The mid-points are what the lower points become if taken to extremes.

Virtue: Endurance – *"Blessed are those who endure, for they shall have faith."*
Sense: for the *Ego or "I"* of others
World View: Mathematism (*reducing to essentials*), symmetry
Exercise: Control of *feeling* nature

With Gemini there can be extreme mood swings. The exterior outpouring of the *feeling* nature can be given over to outbursts of emotional temper. Often when one is born to a particular sign, it indicates a weakness that needs to be overcome.

Gemini Individuals
Sun in **Gemini**: *"Reveal thyself, Sun life"*
first decan – Jupiter – Orion
Composers Grieg (1°) and Stravinsky (3°), French philosophers Jean-Paul Sartre (6°) and Blaise Pascal (8°).
second decan – Mars – Canis Major (the Greater Dog)
French author Jean-Jacques Rousseau (16°), writers George Sand (18°), Franz Kafka (18°), Hermann Hesse (18°), King James I of England (18°), Italian freedom fighter Guiseppe Garibaldi (19°), German mathematician and philosopher Leibniz (20°) and American novelist Nathaniel Hawthorne (20°).
third decan – Sun – Canis Minor (the Lesser Dog)
Composer Gustav Mahler (22°), Spanish mystic St. John of the Cross (23°), American entrepreneur John D. Rockefeller (24°), American author Saul Bellow (24°), electrical scientist Nikolai Tesla (25°), French authors Marcel Proust (25°) and Jean de la Fontaine (27°), painter Rubens (27°), King Henry VIII of England (27°), and American author Henry David Thoreau (28°).

Cosmic *Eurythmy*
"In the Image and Likeness..."

***Cancer*:** Nurturing

Green – *"Breath of life"*

A major / F# minor[32]

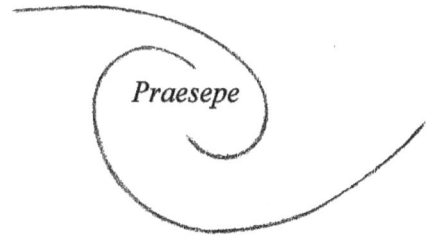

Praesepe

The twinship of Gemini develops further in the realm of Cancer which is the generating force for the formation of the human rib cage. As a furthering of the *sounding* instrument of the collar bone, the ribs spiral out in *pairs* from the twelve vertebrae of the thoracic spinal region. It is through our rib cage that the exquisite refinement of inner life and our attunement to the feeling nature of cosmic realities are made possible.

The human rib cage is like a living, breathing cosmic womb. We can see the streaming in (*inbreath*) and out (*outbreath*) of etheric cosmic forces in the spiraling arms of the astrological sign for Cancer ♋ which mirrors the etheric streaming of the constellation.[33]

The cluster of stars which mark the center or reversal of the two spiraling arms is called **Praesepe**. The Greeks called this cluster of stars the *Beehive*, marking the *heart* of Cancer as the *gateway of birth* into earthly life. The Greeks believed that the human soul entered earthly incarnation through this gateway to gather the golden "nectar" of earthly experience to take back to the *Queen* of the cosmic realm (**Sophia**).

Just as the queen bee resides within the protective structure of the hive, so too the human heart lives within the protective *sounding* chamber of the rib cage, a sounding chamber of heavenly accord.

As we move this form to music written in the key of A major, we imagine ourselves enfolded in the nurturing quality of the color green – a "greening" of soothing etheric streaming, the breathing in and out of etheric life. *"He maketh me to lie down in green pastures. He restoreth my soul"* (*Psalm 23*).

The movement and gestures of the Cancer form mirror the spiraling of the two arms of Cancer and the breathing out of cosmic love with the eurythmy sound "efff". With the spiraling gestures of Cancer, one can experience a furthering of the realm of **Taurus**, in the taking in of the *full round* of *earthly experience*, and **Gemini**, bringing an *attunement* through the *feeling* nature.

---

[32] *Sharp*, the sign # which raises a note one semitone from its natural pitch as part of the key signature. The *key signature* is the group of sharp or flat signs placed after the clef at the beginning of a composition, or after a double bar in the course of it. The sharps or flats of a key signature are effective throughout a composition unless contradicted by a new key signature (see also footnote 38 on page 50).

[33] The shape of the astrological sign for Cancer (♋) consists of two interlocking spirals, one from the left and the other from the right, reminding us of the pairs of ribs making up the rib cage.

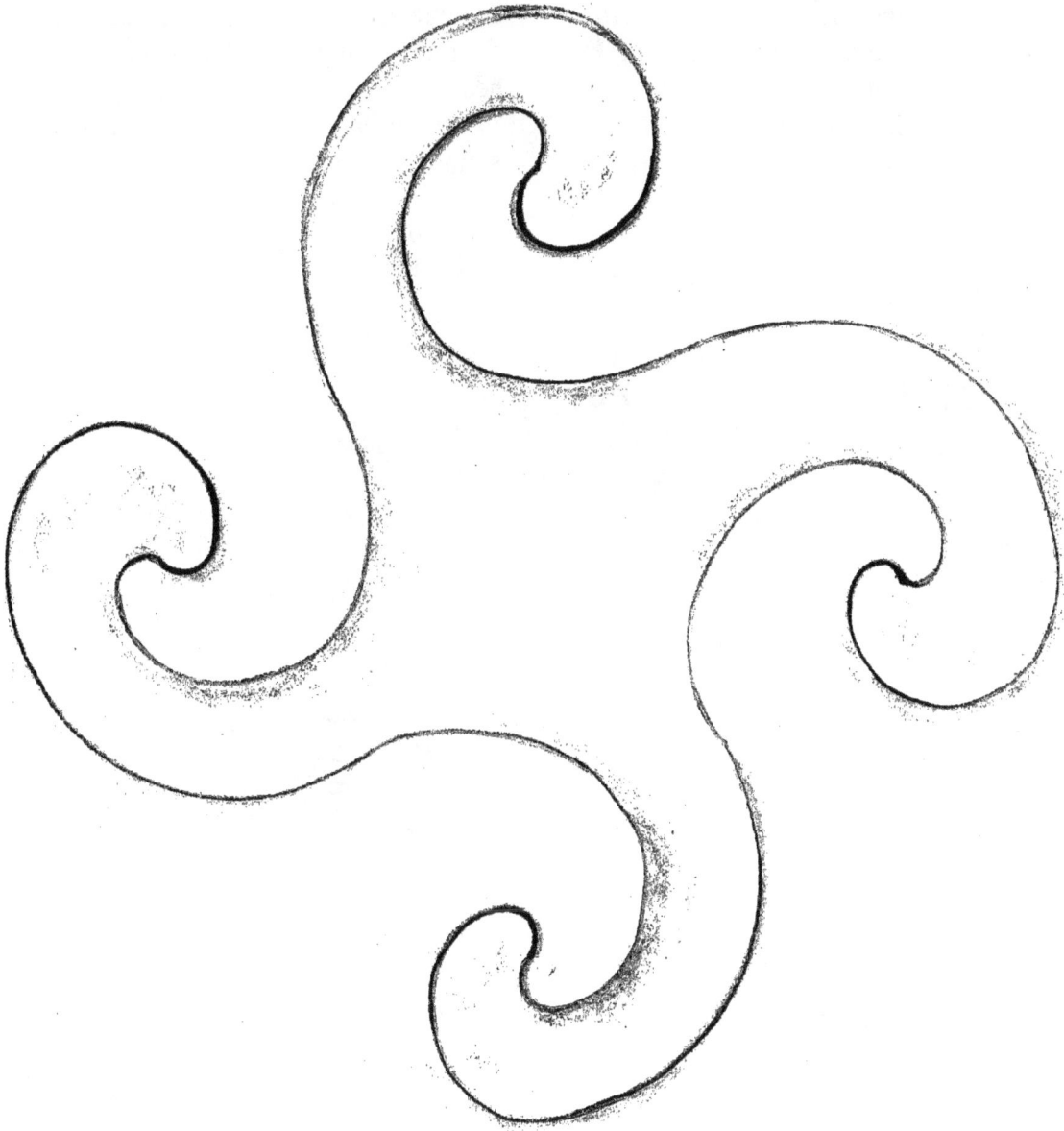

Cancer Choreography

Cancer Cosmic Dance Form
"Transmission of wisdom and positivity"

Cancer *eurythmy* form:

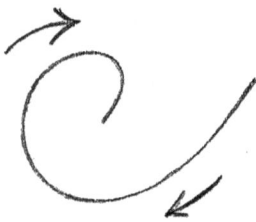

Begin, by circling back to the left, circling around to the right and back to the left, spiraling clockwise into the center of the spiral form.

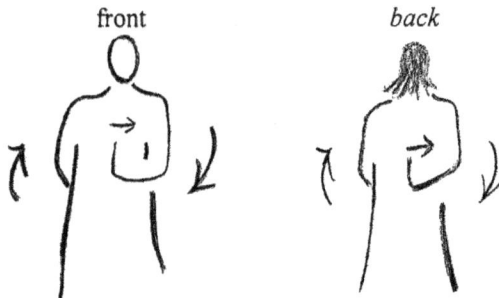

front   back

The second (outward) spiral circles back (*slightly*) to the left, then around to the right counter-clockwise, completing the outward spiral by flowing around further to the left.

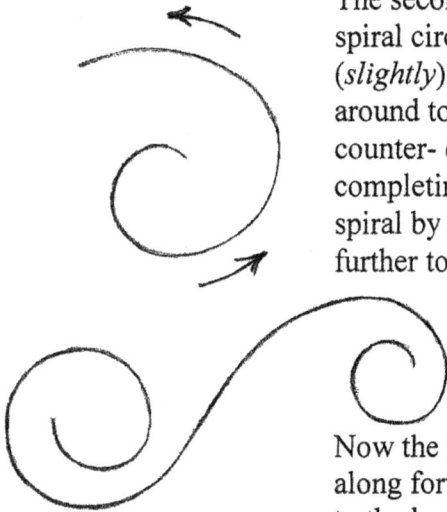

Now the form moves along forward to the left to the beginning point of the next spiraling in...

Continue *Form*: repeat spiraling in and spiraling out, *and feel yourself rocked to and fro in a cosmic sea of etheric nurturing forces.*

Cancer *Gesture*:

As you circle around, the arms move away from the body and circle around to the right, bringing the left hand into the heart center *open palm facing left, fingers extended upward*. The right arm simultaneously flows out and around the body, bringing the right hand to the center of the back *palm open facing right, fingers extended upward*.

On the outward spiral, the arms slowly unfurl, moving out and around forward once again (*heart level*) making ready for the Cancer sound gesture "efff".

Cancer *Sound*: "efff"[34]
While moving forward to the left, arms gesture forward like lightning, palms open, facing earth, as though emitting flashes of cosmic fire from finger tips.

Alternate forming Cancer gesture *on the spiraling in*, releasing the gesture on *the spiraling out*; completing the form with the eurythmy sound "efff" *while moving forward to the left.*

---

[34] "efff" – transmission of wisdom and positivity (sound of Isis).

38

Cancer *"The Crab"* (July 17 – August 18)
"The gathering of the sheep..."

With the star *Procyon* (1°Cancer) on the leading edge of the threshold (cusp) of entry into the constellation of Cancer, we have a telling image for the great work or spiritual intention of **Cancer**, which is all about *redemption*.

Procyon, called the *"Redeemed Redeemer"*, is the speaking force for the constellation of the *Lesser Dog*, **Canis Minor,** whose etheric forces nourish the final region of *The Twins*, where the vitality of the *intellect* is brought into relationship with the *feeling* heart, the work of the "two becoming one".[35]

Here the image of the "Lesser" is important, for we are brought into an understanding of the words of John the Baptist wherein he speaks *"I must become less so that he might become more."* One can anticipate here the beginning stages of a coming into the "Pleroma", the fullness of the birth of the Christ within.

We remember *Praesepe*, the *"Beehive"* cradle at the center of the spiraling in and spiraling out of Cancer and ponder the words of Goethe, " *When the inside is in order, the outside takes care of itself."* Whereas Gemini's relational aspect is all about the "other", knowing oneself through the reflection of the other, clearly Cancer is about the inside-outside relationship – understanding that what lives within is reflected outwardly. This calls forth the "inner work" of redeeming the outer reality.

Like the spiraling arms of Cancer, the stories and myths associated with this region of the heavens bear images of gathering, carrying and the *voyage* home.

The *deck* of the great cosmic ship **Argo**, stretches its starry face across the heavens in this region below Cancer, the *carrying* deck which gathers the seekers of the "Golden Fleece." The Sun at the birth of the Nathan Mary was at 25½° ♋ in the region of the carrying deck of Argo giving us a telling image of Mary's role as co-redeemer for humankind.

The constellations of **Ursa Major** and **Ursa Minor** also grace the region above Cancer. The prominent star configurations within the constellations of Ursa Major and Ursa Minor are known as the *Big Dipper* and *Little Dipper*, and the constellations as a whole are referred to as the Greater and Lesser *Bears* or sometimes as the *Chariots*.

In northern legend the seven stars of the Big Dipper were associated with the "Chariot of Arthur" and the seven stages of *initiation*. Attunement to these stars brings a *sense ability* to know the truth. In Taoist meditation practices, attunement to these stars accompanies one's passage through the seasons in order to facilitate the spiritualization of the human soul.

---

[35] Procyon marks the rear flank of Canis Minor, the Lesser Dog. Most of the stars of Canis Minor are located in the third decan of Gemini, with which the Lesser Dog is associated. However, Procyon, being at the rear end of Canis Minor, is at 1° Cancer, just into Cancer from Gemini.

It is precisely this inspiration which brings us to yet another naming for this constellation which is also known as the "*Plough*", associated with the tilling of the soil, the upturning of the soil (bringing the inside, outside and the outside, inside) bringing fresh air and light to the soil of the soul.

Both the good ship **Argo** and the **Plough** are associated with the *gathering* of the "Flock" or sheep (*the saved ones*) and bringing them back home to the cosmic realm. Perhaps home referred to the "Pole Star", which the two end stars of the Big Dipper point toward.

In the northern lands, the constellations to which the Dippers belong were referred to as the Big Bear and the Little Bear, associated with the myth of ***Jupiter*** being *confined* to a cave to develop his cosmic thinking. According to Aratos the two bears were the nurses of Zeus (Jupiter) in his cave on the island of Crete. The Bears were subsequently raised to heaven for their devotion to Zeus. Jupiter's point of *exaltation* is in the inner sanctum of *Praesepe*,[36] the *Beehive* cradle of Cancer, which is *ruled* by the **Moon**, bringing the gift of reflection.

We find an echo of the story of Jupiter's confinement in the cosmic remembrance of the *imprisonment* of John the Baptist when the Sun stood at 25°Cancer.

As with the form for the cosmic dance of Cancer, with these myths one feels oneself carried on an ocean of etheric love.

In the work of transformation there is a movement from one's own small house (Ego) into the larger house (Higher Self), the house of the *Father*. "*Our Father's house has many mansions.*" So it is with the *Crab*, which outgrows its shell.

---

[36] The Babylonians depicted on a cuneiform text Jupiter exalted in Praesepe. In listing the zodiacal degree of Jupiter's exaltation as 15°♋ the question is whether actually 12½°♋ is meant, which is the longitude of Praesepe.

Cancer Meditation Work: *"Selflessness becomes catharsis..."*

Sun in Cancer: July 17 – August 18

Cancer is ruled by the Moon and is associated with the breast region of the human being. Thus, Cancer is thought of as the "Mother sign" of the Zodiac rendering a tender nurturing quality.

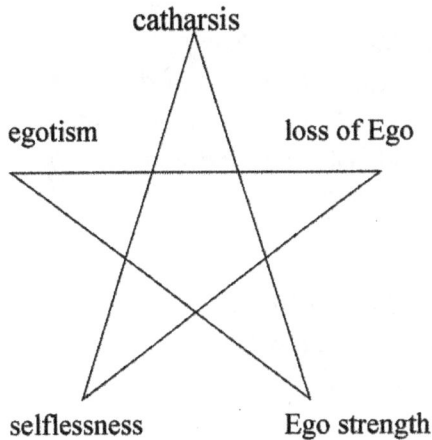

catharsis

egotism   loss of Ego

selflessness   Ego strength

We can imagine the rib cage as a *safe haven* – the *receptive cradle* for the birth of the Christ within the human heart.

The exquisite feeling nature emanating from the realm of Cancer renders a sense of *sense ability* which is both gift and challenge.

The sensing organ of the rib cage renders a sense for the interiority of things, the *inner being* nature of the world.

The lower two points provide the foundation required to achieve the higher aspect of Cancer. The lower left-hand corner is the virtue. The lower right-hand corner is what is needed along with the virtue in order to arrive at the uppermost point. The mid-points are what the lower points become if taken to extremes.

Sense: Touch

World View: Materialism
In the higher sense, it is an appreciation for matter as the foundation for material existence. Matter and mother have the same root in Latin (mother = *mater*; matter = *materia*). Herein lies a challenge, for the material world view can bring a hardening aspect to the tender skin (thin skin) of the feeling nature of Cancer.

Ideal: The washing of the feet.
The instinct to purify oneself – the Cathars were the "pure ones".

Sun in **Cancer**: *"Thou resting, glowing light."*

Mary of Nazareth was born when the Sun was located at 25½°Cancer, on the outstreaming arm of the etheric *breath* of the Crab. Thus, the archetype of *Motherhood* was cradled in the heart of Cancer.

Another archetypal example of the Cancer individuality is the disciple James the Elder, who represents *Hope*. [Peter – Taurus (*Faith*), John – Gemini (*Love*), and James – Cancer (*Hope*) were the three disciples who witnessed the *transfiguration* of Jesus Christ on Mount Tabor.]

Other significant **Cancer** individuals

first decan – Mercury – Argo Navis (the Ship Argo – Puppis, the Stern)
Founder of Christian Science Mary Baker Eddy (2˚), painters Chagall (3˚) and
Rembrandt (3˚), author Ernest Hemingway (5˚), Reformation theologian Calvin (9˚),
psychologist Jung (10˚), playwright George Bernard Shaw (10½˚).

second decan – Venus – Ursa Minor (the Lesser Bear – the Neck of the Bear)
United Nations General Secretary Dag Hammarskjold (12˚), English poet Gerard Manley
Hopkins (13˚), Italian dictator Mussolini (13˚), sculptor Henry Moore (14˚), automobile
manufacturer Henry Ford (14˚), writer Emily Brontë (14½˚), Russian St. Seraphim (16˚),
author Herman Melville (16˚), Italian poet Petrarch (19½˚), French writer Guy de
Maupassant (20˚).

third decan – Moon – Ursa Major (the Greater Bear – the Flank of the Bear)
English poets Tennyson (21˚) and Shelly (21˚), Russian founder of the Theosophical
Society H. P. Blavatsky (26˚), yoga teacher Sri Aurobindo (29½˚).

Cosmic *Eurythmy*
"In the Image and Likeness…"

Leo – Enthusiasm

Blue (royal) *"In devotion the soul finds itself"*

E major/C# minor

Regulus

The region of the fixed stars known as Leo provide the archetypal pattern for the shaping and functioning of the human heart and circulatory system. Nestled within the protective cradle of the rib cage formed through the forces of Cancer, we experience a further refining of the divine *inbreath*.

The inner alchemy of the human heart functions to transform the condition of the blood, to "temper" the incoming *sound* quality (*inbreath*/*venous blood*) before *breathing* out once more supplying the circulatory system with the wine of *vitality,* freshly oxygenated arterial blood.

The human heart functions as the *inner Sun* for the human being, just as our Sun brings life to our solar system. Correspondingly, the Great Central Sun, the fiery *heart* of the galaxy, brings life to our Sun and the galaxy.

The functioning of the human heart mirrors the rhythm of the cosmic heart. The 72 beats per minute of the heart correspond to the movement of the vernal point through one degree of the zodiac in 72 years.

We can see the circulatory system mirrored in the pattern of the etheric streaming of Leo, streaming in from the tail of the *Lion* and circling around the form of the Lion's heart, which is marked by the great star ***Regulus*** (5°Leo).

The eurythmy form for Leo mirrors the etheric streaming of the constellation. We can recall the *kingly* nature of the *Lion* as we imagine ourselves immersed in the *royalty* of the color blue.

With the Leo gesture we trace the magnificent heavenly realm of Leo, as our arms rise forming the majesty of the *Lion's* mane. From our heart streams the radiance of the Sun, which we experience as *"the raying in of spirit"* with the final crowning gesture of the eurythmy sound "T".

As we dance the cosmic dance of Leo, we trace the etheric streaming of the astrological sign (♌) while at the same time honoring the miracle of the human circulatory system which flows from the heart out to the extremities and back again to the heart.

43

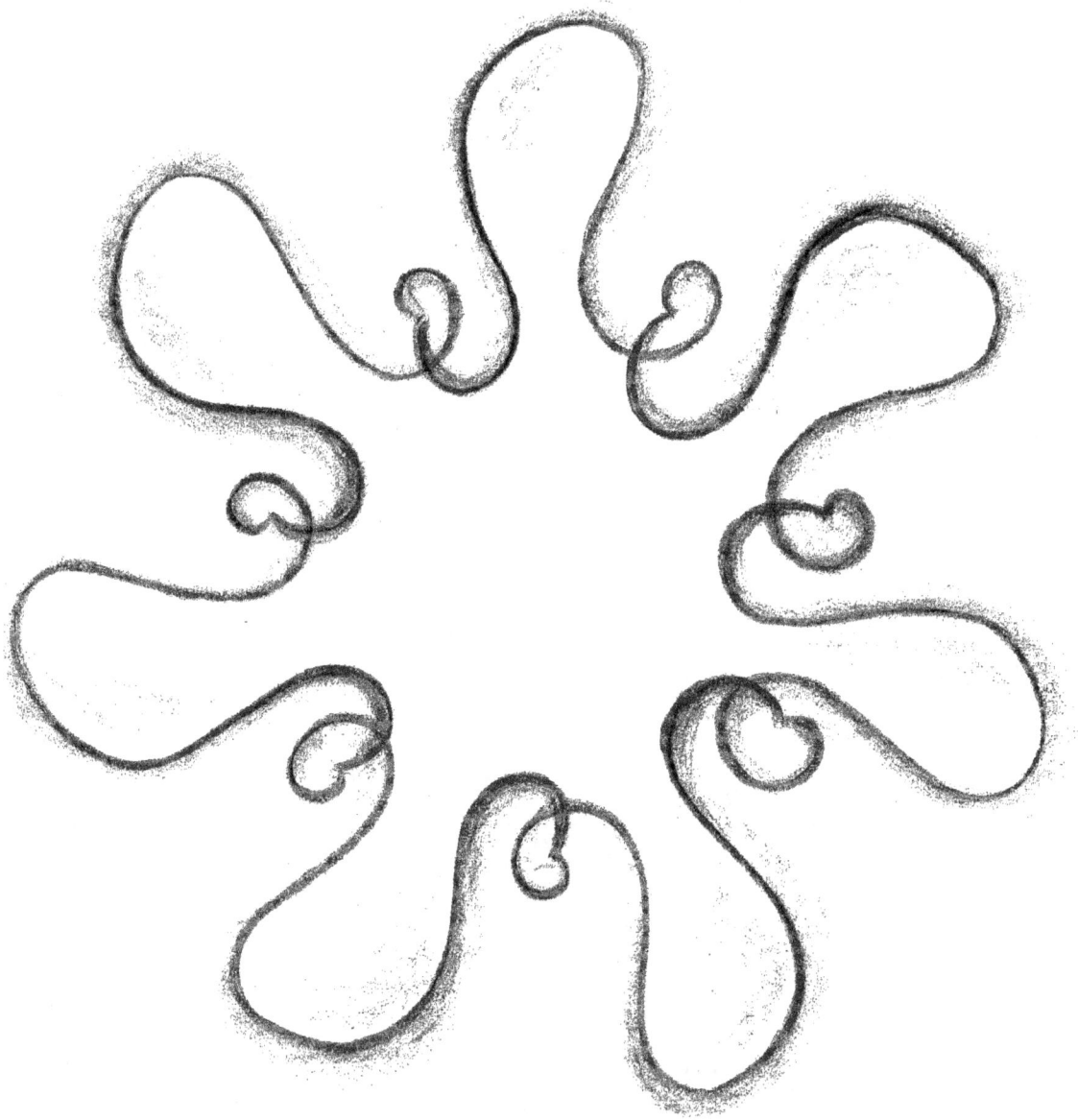

Leo Choreography

Leo Cosmic Dance Form
"The raying in of spirit"

Leo *Eurythmy* Form:

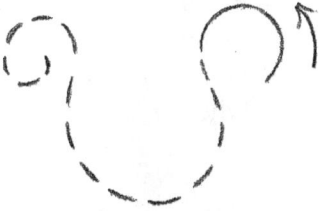

Begin by moving in a small curve forward and to the left, forming the tail of the Lion.

Then *a more sweeping movement* curving back *slightly* to the right, then curving around and making a large curve to the left *forming the back of the Lion.*

Then a *sweeping movement* forward, curving *slightly* to the right, and then circling around forward to the left, spiraling *counter clockwise* into the heart of the Lion.

Continue form: Curving forward to the left *out from the center*, forming the Leo gesture on the movement back and the sound "T" on the movement spiraling in *forming the heart of the Lion.*

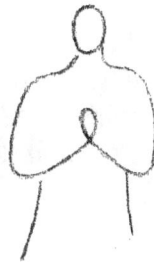

Forming the Lion's Mane

"T"

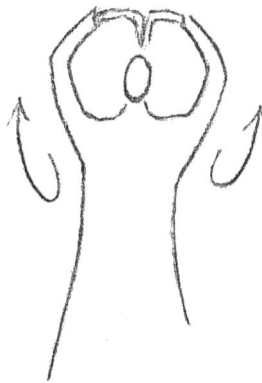

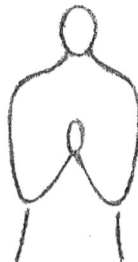

Leo *Gesture*:
While moving the tail form of Leo, bring hands to the heart center, left hand gently cupped, right hand covering left.

While moving back, arms flow out to the side moving *upwards* and opening out above the head. *Fingers <u>stretched</u> wide, palms open facing <u>out</u> away from body* – completing gesture at the back of the circle *raying out from the heart.*

Leo *Sound*: "T"
While moving forward arms are released and flow down, then they are lifted up (*palms open/facing up*) and curve in above the head *while spiraling around the Lion's heart.*

Backs of hands come together, fingers down, above the center of crown, pause and drop gently to touch the crown with finger tips, *completing this gesture as you spiral into the heart of the Lion.*

Releasing the "T" gesture, lower arms to heart level, hands gently cupped over heart chakra *to begin next Leo form.*

Leo   "The Lion"   (August 18 – September 17)
"...the region of the birth of the Sun."

The star **Regulus** (5°Leo) which marks the heart of the *Lion* is one of the "Four Royal Stars" which form a cross in the heavens. Regulus was called by the ancients, the "Watcher in the North"[37] and is associated with the "*Lion of Judah*," designating the line of descent from King David, including the *Solomon* (kingly) stream and the *Nathan* (priestly) stream.

King David's line of descent made possible the birth of both the *Solomon* Jesus and the *Nathan* Jesus. There is no doubt that the four Royal Stars have something to do with the "royal way", a path of initiation which has to do with true kingship, the *transformed heart*. The royal mast of the celestial ship **Argo** points in the direction of the star **Regulus** reminding us of Christ gathering his flock for the voyage home.

The human heart (the Christ center of the human being) and circulatory system remind us of this faithful, steady promise, through the reviving process of receiving the venous life (oxygen depleted blood), sending it to the lungs for new breath, receiving it once more to be re-circulated through the arteries and tiny capillary systems which vivify the human form.

Leo is said to be the region of the birth of the Sun. Just as the Sun is the *heart* of the *solar system* bringing life to earth, so too the human *heart* (formed by Leo) brings life to the human being. (Correspondingly on the galactic level the Great Central Sun, the *heart* of the *galaxy,* brings life to the Sun of our solar system.) *"He who is in the fire, and he who is here in the heart and he who is yonder in the Sun, he is one"(Matrihpanishad 6:17).*

The mast of the great ship **Argo** ("*Argus*") points toward the star **Alphard** (2½°Leo) "*the Solitary One*", which marks the *heart* of the cosmic serpent **Hydra**. We think of the intertwining snakes of the *caduceus*, the symbol of healing, when we see the name of **Hydra**, the *Serpent*. Does the rising up of the serpent represent the transformed, spiritualized soul?

Does "kingship" have to do with the overcoming of death? **2½° Leo** marks the cosmic remembrance of the *Conversation at Jacob's well*, wherein Jesus proclaimed the Cosmic Christ as the *source* of eternal life, with **3°Leo** marking the place of the Sun during the *raising of Lazarus from the dead*. This beginning decan of Leo is *ruled* by Saturn.

This region of the Lion also remembers the *healing of the Nobleman's Son* (10½°Leo), brought about through the re-assumption of the nobleman's *sovereignty* which had been given over to an earthly master. This is an archetypal image for the transformed heart and the birth of the Sun within the human being.

---

[37] Fomalhaut, located 21° south of the ecliptic, was the "Watcher in the South", associated with Aquarius (opposite Leo). Fomalhaut (9°♒) marks the mouth of the Southern Fish receiving the stream of water pouring out from the Waterman's Urn.

If we expand our awareness, we see the *fullness* of the sails of the great ship **Argo** lending *redeemed* etheric life to the *body* of **Leo** which also holds the memory of the deaths of the two Marys, 12½° ♌ marking the death of the *Nathan* Mary in 12 AD and 22½° ♌ the death of the *Solomon* Mary in Ephesus in 44 AD.

The fully engulfed sails of the ship **Argo** mirror the functioning of the lungs in the human being to cleanse and purify the blood, providing freshly oxygenated blood for the arteries, *new wine* for the body, in service to the organ of the heart. We think of the heart in the human being in correspondence to the Sun in the solar system.

Just as the serpent sheds its skin in the process of growth, so too we must be transformed in order to provide a new *wineskin* for the fresh wine of *eternal life*.

Leo Meditation work: *"Compassion becomes freedom"*

Sun in Leo: August 18 – September 17

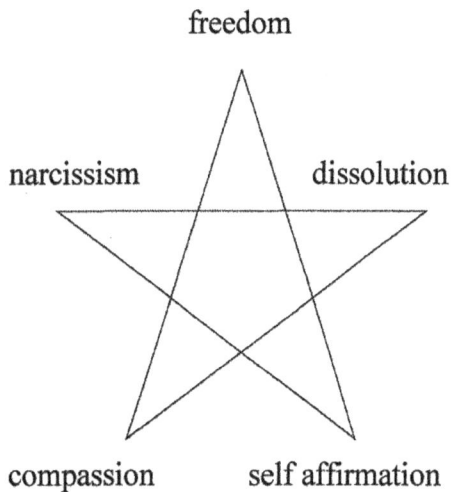

freedom

narcissism   dissolution

compassion   self affirmation

Having a heart for life is the challenge of Leo.

How not to overwhelm another with one's own *inflated* sense of self importance.

How not to lay claim to another's life forces in order to enhance one's own sense of self empowerment.

The lower two points provide the foundation required to achieve the higher aspect of Leo. The lower left-hand corner is the virtue. The lower right-hand corner is what is needed along with the virtue in order to arrive at the uppermost point. The mid-points are what the lower points become if taken to extremes.

Virtue: Compassion – *"Blessed are the compassionate for they shall be free."*

Ideal: *"Not I, but Christ in me..."*

Sense: **Life** – Leo brings the visceral *sense* for life. Through the circulatory system, one can experience the quality of life in one's own "*kingdom*". The experience of one's own vitality undergoes a *metamorphosis* into the experience of Christ as the bearer of life.

World view: Sensationalism or sensualism

Leo Exercise: "Kingship", the spiritualized **Ego**

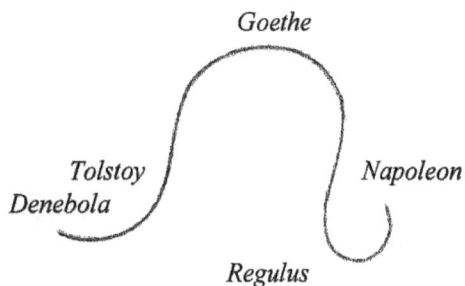

Goethe

Tolstoy
Denebola   *Napoleon*

Regulus

Highest level is when the kingly nature is combined with humility.
Lower aspect of kingship is *power*; higher aspect is *service*.

Leo Individuals

Sun in **Leo**: *"Irradiate with senses' might"*

Tolstoy was born when the Sun was at the *tail* of the Lion (25°). His writings were always reaching out, connecting with the life around him – then drawing it near, feeling its quality in his heart. We might say that this region of Leo inspired Tolstoy's telling of *tales* (stories).

Goethe's natal Sun was in the *fullness* of the Lion's back (14°). He brought his own sense of *sovereignty* and fullness of purpose to life, the full flowering of his life has been of lasting value and influence.

Napoleon (1°) was influenced by the lower aspect of Leo. (Egocentricity)

Among the disciples, James the Lesser provides the archetypal representation for Leo. James the Lesser was quite handsome and was said to look like Jesus. He was a nephew of Jesus.

Other significant **Leo** Individuals

first decan – Saturn – Leo Minor (the Lesser Lion)
Lawrence of Arabia (0½°), Scottish writer Walter Scott (1°), Emperor Franz Joseph I (2½°), composers Stockhausen (5°) and Debussy (6°), King Ludwig II of Bavaria (9°).

second decan – Jupiter – Ursa Major (the Tail of the Great Bear)
German philosopher, theologian and poet Herder (12°), German philosopher Hegel (12½°), nuclear physicist Ernest Rutherford (13°), educator Maria Montessori (15°), writer Arthur Koestler (19°), composer Anton Bruckner (19°).

third decan – Mars – Canes Venatici (the Hunting Dogs)
French general and politician Lafayette (22½°), composer Anton Dvorak (23°), the "Sun King" Louis XIV of France (23°), Tsar Ivan the Terrible (23°), poet Clemens Brentano (24°), Blessed Anne Catherine Emmerich (24°), discoverer of electricity Galvani (25½°), writer D. H. Lawrence (25½°), astronomer Sir James Jeans (26°), philosopher John Locke (26½°), chemist and theologian J. B. Priestley (27°), French politician Cardinal Richelieu (27½°), pianist and composer Clara Schumann (27½°).

Virgo: Sobriety

♍ Indigo *"I find Divine Being in indigo"*

B major / A♭ minor[38]

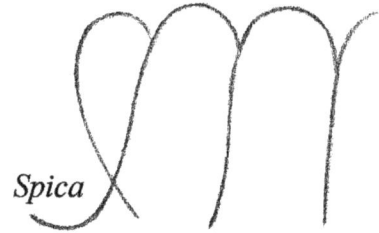

Spica

The region of the constellation of **Virgo** is the formative force for the shape and function of the human digestive system – the internal organs, principally the stomach and small intestinal regions, and the outforming of our musculature. It is through our musculature that we have a sense for movement. And we recognize our movement as a gift of love.

Virgo was seen by the ancient clairvoyants as a young woman holding an ear of corn or sheaf of wheat which is marked by the star ***Spica*** (29°Virgo). Thus, we associate Virgo with the Divine Feminine, the harvest and the bearing of fruit.

We see in the etheric flowing of the celestial stars which shape Virgo a beautiful form that suggests perfection (being almost symmetrical *around its middle axis*). Likewise, the Virgo realm renders an inspiration for *perfection* in form, an *exacting* quality and a *sobering* attention to detail.

The *Solomon* Mary was born when the Sun was in Virgo (16°Virgo), bringing an archetypal sign for celestial perfection, the *wisdom* stream of creation associated with **Isis** and **Sophia**. The *Solomon* Mary is referred to as the "Virgin Mary", who *since her assumption into heaven* is called the Queen of Heaven.

The Virgo eurythmy form is an *artistic* tracing of the zodiacal sign of Virgo ♍, somewhat *metamorphosed*. With the Virgo eurythmy *sound* "B", the arms form the shape of an embrace, which suggests the embrace of the ***Virgin*** holding the *divine child*. In Egyptian iconography **Isis** was depicted sitting holding the child **Horus**, associated with *wisdom*. We see these cosmic mysteries expressed in the astrological sign for "Virgo" where the glyph shows the small rounded arm of the *Virgin* ♍ enfolded in a gesture of embrace.

---

[38] *Flat*, the sign ♭ which lowers a note one semitone from its natural pitch as part of the key signature. The *key signature* is the group of sharp or flat signs placed after the clef at the beginning of a composition, or after a double bar in the course of it. The sharps or flats of a key signature are effective throughout a composition unless contradicted by a new key signature (see also footnote 32 on page 36).

With Virgo, we begin to experience our shape, our outer form (*musculature*) from within, as we consciously sculpt in etheric space the eurythmy *sound* "B". We can imagine *Sophia* opening her starry robes to embrace creation.

As the sixth sign Virgo stands in the middle between that which has come before (past) and that which is yet to come (future), so that the "B" can be experienced as a *gathering* gesture, a bringing together of past and future.

The eurythmy *gesture* for Virgo brings to expression the process of integration. That which the head (Aries) thinks, the nature of our inner life hears (Taurus) and feels (Gemini and Cancer), and that which the heart (Leo) has lived now must be *digested*[39] (Virgo). *Word* has become food, the *harvest* of what has been sown must now be reaped.

Ancient zodiacal drawings picture Virgo as a standing figure with her left arm reaching out towards the tail of Leo, the Lion. Leo (*Fire* sign) relates to the *Father* principle, being ruled by the Sun, the *heart* of our *solar system*; and the *heart* of the *human being* corresponds to Leo. Analogously, Virgo relates to the earth (*Earth* sign), to the very *heart* of *Mother Earth*, and to the *womb* or *bowels* of the earth; and the *digestive tract* of the *human being* corresponds to Virgo. Virgo then becomes the fecund, fertile ground for the forces which generate from the Sun (Christ). We see this mystery enigmatically expressed in the Egyptian Sphinx, with the body of a lion leading to the head of an upright woman, the wisdom of creation (*Sophia*).

As we move the eurythmy form for Virgo, we imagine ourselves embraced in a mantle of celestial indigo blue (*Sophia's robes*). Inwardly carrying the words "I find Divine Essence in indigo", we form the gesture for the sound "B" as we dance to music written in the key of B major or A♭ minor.

---

[39] The small intestines are considered to be the secondary organ of the heart (formed in Leo and *cradled* in the ribcage formed by Cancer); the large intestines are considered to be the secondary organ of the lungs (formed in Gemini). Virgo then is the culminating influence of each of the previous stages. The function of digestion brings thinking and feeling into the *fruition of integration.*

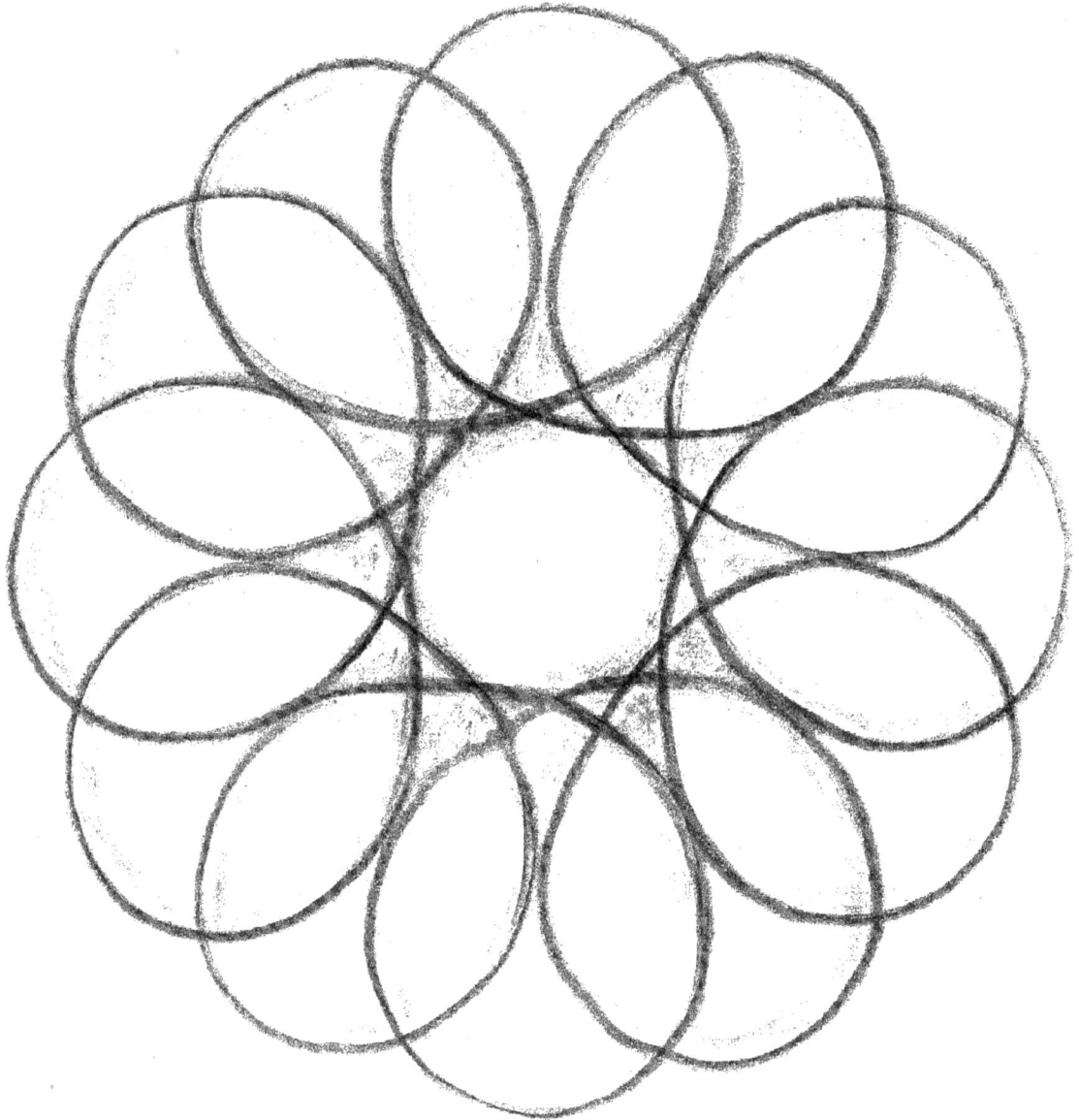

Virgo Choreography

Virgo Cosmic Dance Form
"Embracing the world with love"

Virgo *Eurythmy* Form:

Begin: standing at the backward point of the first loop of the Virgo form *with the Virgo gesture*

Loop forward *slightly* to the right, then circle around *counter clockwise* to the left, *forming the sound "B"*.

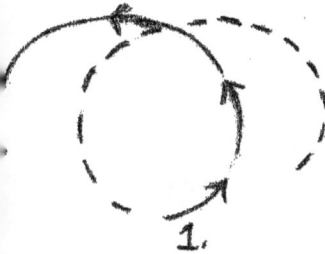

Then loop back *slightly* to the left, releasing the "B" gesture and begin forming the Virgo gesture.

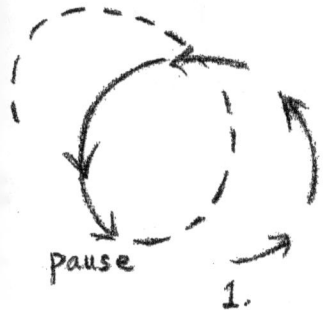

Pause at the completion point of the first loop having completed *forming the Virgo gesture.*

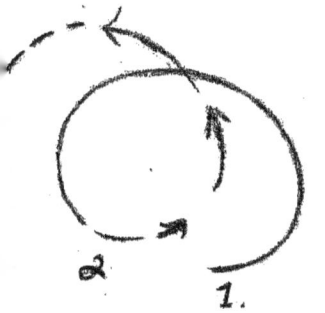

Make a second loop forward *slightly* to the right, circling around *counter-clockwise* to the left, *forming the "B" sound gesture.*

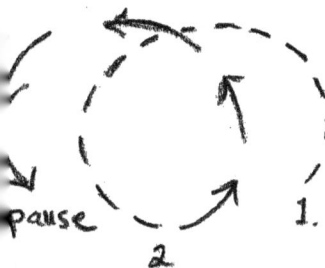

Then, continuing around the loop, *while moving backward* form the Virgo gesture.

Virgo *gesture*:

The left palm slanting downward rests on the left side of the abdomen, while the right arm and hand remain relaxed, extended down the right side.

Virgo *Sound*: "B"

Right arm circles up to heart level; simultaneously left arm circles in toward solar plexus (palms open facing in toward body). This is *an embracing gesture like a mother holding a child*

Repeat the Virgo *gesture* (left hand slanting downward touching left side of abdomen, and right arm extended down) *at the completion of the first loop.*

Virgo *sound*: "B"

Form "B" gesture *reversing the arms*, with the left arm (*palm open*) facing the heart, and the right arm with palm facing the solar plexus.

*Continue the **Virgo form**, forming the "B" gesture alternately with each loop, and the Virgo gesture at the completion point of each loop.*

Virgo – *"Queen of Heaven"* (September 17 – October 18)

Legends and myths connected with the constellation of **Virgo** are ripe with images of the Divine Feminine. The young woman holding a sheaf of wheat was imagined in Egypt as *Isis*, who formed the *"Milky Way"* by dropping wheat across the sky or pouring out milk.

Spica (29° ♍), which marks the tip of the sheaf of wheat, was recognized for its brilliance and its appearance in the night sky during springtime. It inspired the orientation of the temple of Min in Thebes and the temple of the Sun in Tel el-Amarna.

In the Euphrates region, **Virgo** was imagined as *Ishtar*, *"Daughter* of Heaven" and *"Queen* of the Stars". In India, she was called the *"Mother* of Krishna" and the Middle Ages knew her as the *"Virgin* Mary".

In Peru, Virgo was associated with magic and was known as the *"Harvest* Goddess" or *"Earth Mother"*, while the Greeks and Romans associated her with *Persephone* and the depths of the earth. The title "Goddess of the Harvest" was appropriate, considering that the Sun passed through the sign of Virgo at the time of the harvest.

If we gather up these images in the spirit of harvest, we can experience a recognition, a gnosis (direct knowing) of the depth and breadth of Sophia's realm. **Sophia**, the divine Mother of Creation, holy *wisdom*, was known to the ancient world. A pre-figuring of an understanding of the Divine Feminine Trinity – *Mother, Daughter, Holy Soul* – was present in *seed* form in the consciousness of ancient humanity.

In these images we recognize that the *gift* of the harvest was imagined as *rooted* in the stars and that the *work* of the harvest was to *descend*. This is the working of *Persephone*, toward the *harvest* of creation. In the story of Persephone we have a prefiguring of the awareness that is expressed in the *"Our Mother"* prayer, in which there is an acknowledgement of the Mother's descent into the heart of the Earth.[40]

The *heart* of Mother Earth brings an imagination of the mother's womb, fertility, the ability to bear fruit, and to create.

The image of Virgo as the "Virgin" calls to our awareness the *"virginal"* quality, essential to creation and the purity of form, for the *birthing* waters must become *still* (sobriety) in order to reflect inspiration from above without distortion.

Thus, the fiery enthusiasm inspired by the region of **Leo** comes "home to roost", so to speak. **Virgo** ushers in the need to *incubate* and *hold*, to *integrate* experiences, in order to bear the "horn of plenty" and the "harvest of grace".

---

[40] See *Study Material on the Prayer Sequence* for the "Our Mother" prayer in the sacred dance of eurythmy, available from the Sophia Foundation of North America.

Zaniah – "Heaven's Gate"

"When there were no depths, I was brought forth." "Blessed is the man that heareth me, watching daily at my gates." (Sophia – Proverbs 8:24, 34)

16°Virgo marks the birth place of the *Solomon* Mary, referred to in the later Christian tradition as the "Queen of Heaven." Thus, the Sun at Mary's birth had just passed the region of Virgo known to the Chinese as "Heaven's Gate" marked by the star **Zaniah** (10°Virgo), which is located on the Virgin's left arm which carries and holds the vine –*"I am the true vine"*. The Dendera Zodiac of ancient Egypt pictures this left arm reaching toward the tail of the Lion of Leo, associated with the "Lion of Judah". The right arm *holds* the ear of corn / sheaf of *wheat* marked by Spica (29° ♍) –*"I am the bread of life"*.

Zaniah means the "left-hand maintainer of law" and marks the point on the celestial equator which is associated with the mysteries of birth and the laws that govern this gateway.

Might this point toward the meaning of the sphinx who silently waits as the riddle of reason and wisdom? To begin each day in a *virginal* field will harvest the most fertile thinking. Then we can rise with power and might on the wings of the heart and the Lion.

The Feminine Mysteries

When we think of images associated with the Divine Feminine, we think of the themes of *temptation* (the serpent), *intuition* (feminine wisdom), and the *womb* (vessel, Grail).

Thus, it is not surprising to find the *body* of **Hydra** "the Serpent" stretching its undulating life force throughout the entire region beneath Virgo. Here we have the story of the temptation of Eve represented by the words, *"The serpent was more cunning and tempted the human soul."* And with these words come the promise of the role of *intuition* and the *womb*, the Grail promise, *"I will put enmity between you (serpent) and the woman, and between your seed and her seed; he shall bruise your head, and you shall bruise his heel."*

The constellation of the **Crater** "the Cup" – a Grail symbol – is balanced on the undulating form of the serpent along with **Corvus** "the Raven", a symbol for the intelligence of feminine wisdom, the ability to understand right timing (*Noah* sent a raven to check out the lay of the land) and of the quality of receptivity (*vessel/womb*) necessary to receive divine guidance. A raven brought bread to Elijah, the daily bread of existence, symbolized by the sheaf of wheat in the Virgin's right hand.

These images *balancing* on the undulating form of the serpent's body, the **Cup** (*Grail*) and the **Raven** (*intuition*), remind us of yet another embodiment of the Divine Feminine, **Kwan Yin**, the Goddess of Compassion. Kwan Yin is depicted in art as *balancing* on the back of the sea serpent of *temptation,* which represents the flowing constancy of the life of the soul. Kwan Yin provides an archetypal image of balance and harmony which is both grace-filled (Holy Grail) and gracious (divine wisdom).

55

Virgo Meditation Work: *"Courtesy becomes tact of heart"*

Sun in Virgo: September 17 – October 18

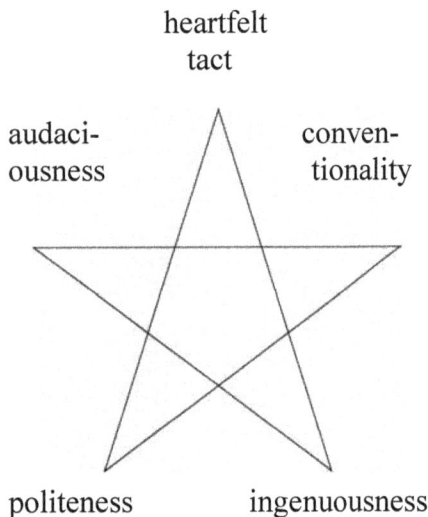

```
              heartfelt
                tact

audaci-                    conven-
ousness                      tionality




politeness        ingenuousness
```

Virgo is called the "House of Mercury",[1] due to the mercurial, *quicksilver* quality that it brings to the human temperament.

The inner work of descent presented in the image of Persephone is important in order to bring awareness to the surface, an opportunity toward self knowledge to "unearth" the fruits of the harvest.

Self-knowledge is an important antidote to the inclination toward harsh judgement of others. This is the work of developing the ability to acknowledge imperfection as a mirroring of one's own unredeemed qualities.

The lower two points provide the foundation required to achieve the higher aspect of Virgo. The lower left hand corner is the virtue. The lower right hand corner is what is needed along with the virtue in order to arrive at the uppermost point. The mid-points are what the lower points become if taken to extremes.

Virtue: Courtesy – *"Blessed are the courteous, for they shall have tact of heart."*

Sense: Movement – (coming from the inner experience of one's own musculature).

Virgo Individuals:
Sun in **Virgo**: *"Behold worlds, O soul!"*

The disciple Bartholomew is the archetypal representative of the constellation of Virgo. Bartholomew is described by Anne Catherine Emmerich as an elegant, refined scribe. He was martyred by being skinned alive and, according to some, reincarnated as Michelangelo. In the monumental painting of the "Last Judgment" by Michelangelo, Bartholomew is shown holding his own skin whose face is clearly identifiable as the face of Michelangelo.

The Virgo influence brings an appreciation for the perfection of form. Human form is exquisitely felt *within* the musculature of the human being. The great painter and sculptor Michelangelo was inspired by the beauty of the human form. He painted the grandeur of the human form on the ceiling of the Sistine Chapel at the Vatican, telling the story of creation as a gift from the heavens above.

---

[1] Virgo (Earth sign) is ruled by Mercury, whose quickening effect is received as the maturity (wisdom) of fine wine as compared to the spirited liveliness (Air sign) of Gemini, which is also ruled by Mercury. The planet Mercury is also exalted at 15° Virgo.

Significant **Virgo** individuals

first decan – Sun – Crater (the Cup)
Composer Gustav Holst (5°), science-fiction writer H. G. Wells (5½°), Queen Elizabeth I
of England (6°), physicist Michael Faraday (7½°), composer Shostakovich (8°), Roman
Emperor Caligula (8½°), Richard the Lionheart (9°).

second decan – Mercury – Corvus (the Raven)
German philosopher Martin Heidegger (10½°), poet T. S. Eliot (10½°), Pope Paul VI
(11°), animal experimenter Pavlov (11°), General Wallenstein (12°), atomic physicist
Enrico Fermi (12½°), French Premier Clemenceau (13°), Caspar Hauser (14°), British
admiral Lord Nelson (15°), Theosophist leader Annie Besant (15°), Mahatma Gandhi
(16°).

third decan – Venus – Hydra (the Serpent – Tail of the Serpent)
Savonarola (20½°), Danish physicist Niels Bohr (21°), French encyclopedist Denis
Diderot (21°), Norwegian explorer Fridtjof Nansen (24°), composer Guiseppe Verdi
(25°), Swiss poet Conrad Ferdinand Meyer (25½°), philosopher and theologian Edith
Stein (25½°), Italian painter Caravaggio (26°), art patron Cosimo di Medici (26°), Italian
painter Tintoretto (27°), American poet E. E. Cummings (28°), German philosopher
Friedrich Nietzsche (29½°), English poet and playwright Oscar Wilde (29½°).

Cosmic *Eurythmy*
"In the Image and Likeness of..."

Libra – Balance

Violet – *"The immeasurable realm of eternity shines"*

F# major/Gb major/D# minor/Eb minor

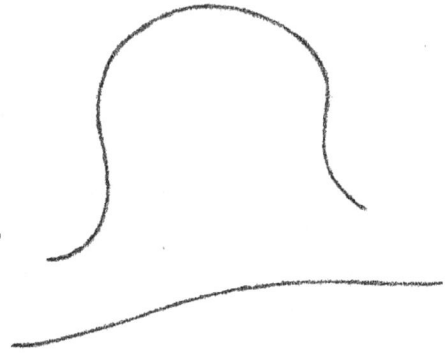

The etheric stream which flows through the region of fixed stars known as **Libra** forms the shape of two "balance pans" connected on either side to a ballast or central fulcrum. We see this form mirrored in the formation of the human hips, which are held in balance by the upright alignment of the human spinal column.

This etheric streaming bears the archetypal pattern for the form and functioning of the hips, kidneys and colon of the human being.

To understand the inspiration of Libra, we must understand that the inspiring "ballast" which holds the balance pans in balance is the spiritual function of the element of *air,* which brings the winds of change to *color* the seasons.

This requires the inner and outer activity of the *balance* of one's thought life. The up and down, left and right, heaven and earth, levity and gravity relationships of life, require a harmonizing of the inner will with the forces of change that pulse through our daily lives.

We experience the divine intention of Libra not only in the left/right balance of the hips in our daily walk through life, but also in the "stepped scale" of our vertebrae. The hip girdle not only stabilizes but also encases the vertebrae surrounding the spinal cord, and when in a state of balance brings a sense of *harmony* to the 31 pairs of spinal nerves branching off from the spinal cord, which bring life to enliven the limbs.

The words graceful, order, harmony, equanimity, and justice live in the perfection of our human form. This gift comes with the *response ability* to maintain the *balance*.

We celebrate this sacred promise in the eurythmy dance of Libra. The Libra form traces the etheric flow of the cosmic pattern of Libra.

With the forming of each "balance pan" we move forward toward our earthly life and tasks and lift our thoughts toward heaven with the sound "C" (as in dan*c*e).

Our limbs feel the tension of *response ability*, as they co-operate to maintain our *uprightness* in the movement.

Thus, there is both *tension* and *lightness* in the celebration of the gifts of Libra. (See *Meditations On The Tarot : "Scales of Justice"*.)

Thus, there is both *tension* and *lightness* in the celebration of the gifts of Libra. (See *Meditations on the Tarot*, *Arcanum VIII: the "Scales of Justice".*)

As we shape the supporting fulcrum, we experience the harmony and grace of the human "fulcrum" of our upright vertebrae as the left/ right scales (hips) come into balance with the "stepped scale" of the vertebrae in the human spinal column (fulcrum), while our arms give expression to the eurythmy *sounding* of Libra. [42]

As we reach the midpoint of the fulcrum form, our arms mirror the mediating balance of the fulcrum by coming together in the center with the Libra gesture.

---

[42] "C" (Ts) – becoming light, material lifted to the spiritual, the sound associated with the sign of Libra.

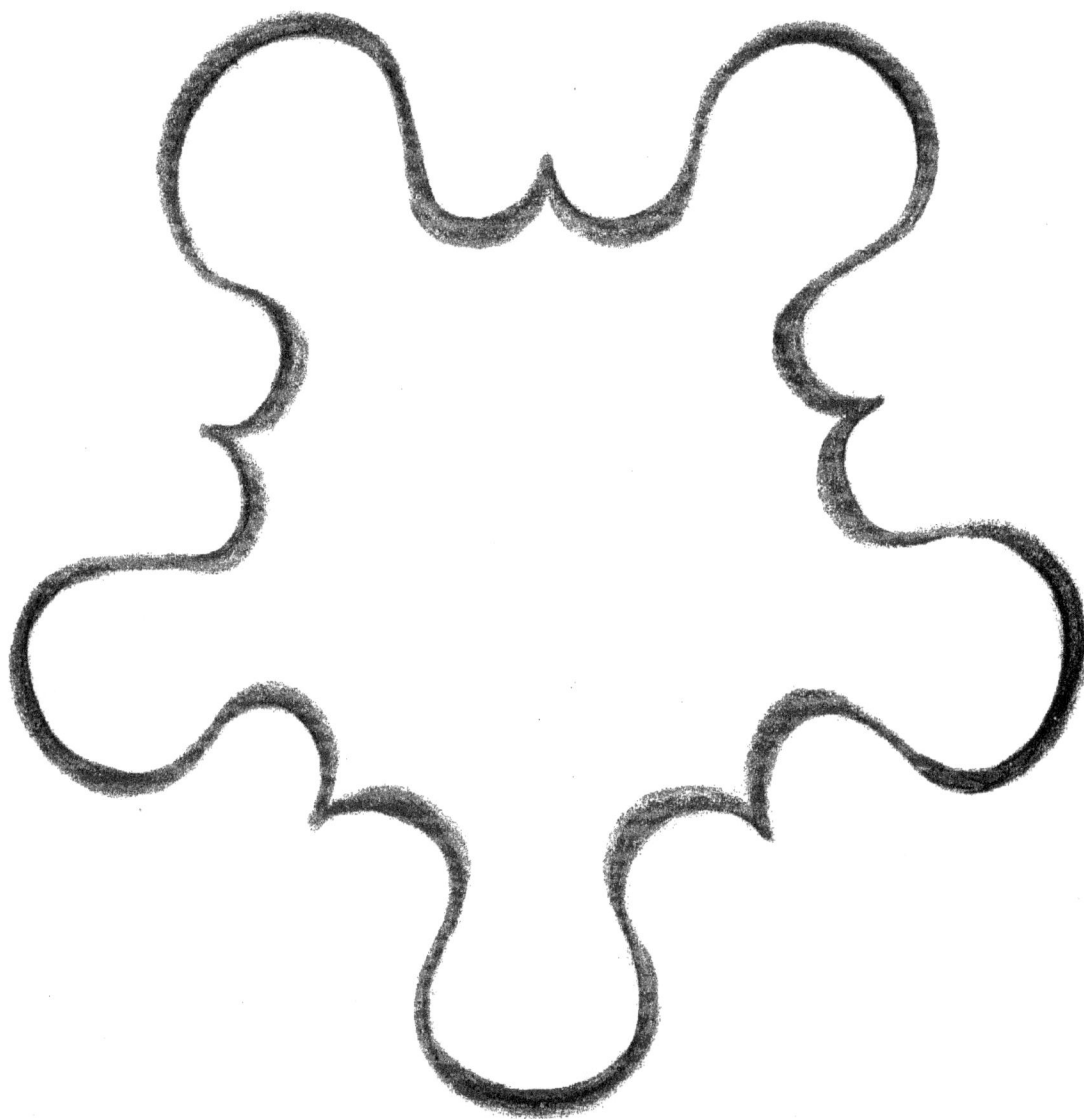

Libra Choreography

Libra Cosmic Dance Form
"Lifting the material into the spiritual"

We imagine ourselves moving in a mist of violet light as we move to music written in the key of F♯ or G♭ major (the major keys corresponding to Libra).

Libra *Form*:
Begin by moving forward and making a small arc to the left – *forming the first balance pan.*

Continue moving back curving to the right and then swinging around to the left, forming the curved beam of the fulcrum part of the scales.

Continue moving forward curving to the right and then…

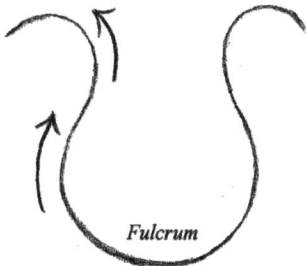

Fulcrum

making a small arc to the left, *form the second balance pan.*

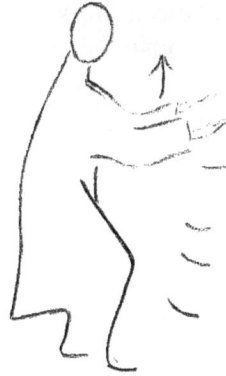

Libra *Sound*: "C"(Ts) *While forming the first balance pan,* sink down at the knees *(keeping erect, not stooping)* while hands scoop down *palms open facing up* as though gathering etheric clouds. Gently moving elbows in and out, lift the palms up in small feather-like gestures, *while returning to erect posture.*

Libra *Gesture*: *While forming the curved beam of the scale,* extend arms forward. Bring right arm to cover left arm, right palm above left palm *palms open facing down.* Form the gesture slowly, completing the gesture at the fulcrum point of the curved beam of the scales.

Hold the gesture *while moving forward* curving in toward the right.

Slowly release the **Libra *gesture*** and repeat the **Libra *sound*** "C"(Ts) *while forming the second balance pan.*

Pause and then begin again to form the first balance pan of the next Libra form.

Libra   *"The Scales"*   (October 18 – November 17)
"The heaped up altar"

The astrological sign (♎) for **Libra** bears the image of an upper and lower bar, a "mirroring" or "as above, so below" image, with a *heaped up* midpoint on the upper bar.

This *heaped up* midpoint mirrors the etheric flowing which shapes the fulcrum of Libra and suggests the inner working of the constellation. This becomes clarified by the reading of the starry script that supports this region of the heavens. Home to both **Corona**, the "*Northern Crown*" (northern hemisphere) and the **Southern Cross** (southern hemisphere), **Libra's** heart is revealed as the work of *atonement*, a building toward the "*Life Spirit*" of the future.

The grouping of stars called the **Southern Cross** reside beneath the hindquarters of **Centaurus**, the "*Centaur*", who carries the "*Sword of Truth*", a Michaelic figure who stretches his starry body throughout the entire region of Libra, thereby bequeathing his etheric forces to this sign. The **Centaur** – half man, half animal – reminds us of Longinus whose spear pierced the right side *through to the heart* of Jesus Christ. The significance of this *fifth wound*, the "wound of the heart", is described in <u>Meditations on the Tarot</u>, <u>Chapter V</u>.

The balancing symbol for this deed of *surrender* on the part of Jesus Christ thus becomes the **Crown** (Corona) of immortal glory, which is the reward in heaven for having first received the "*crown of thorns*". The <u>Moon</u> was full in the heart of Libra at the *crucifixion* on the cross. This is remembered by the **Southern Cross** which stands perpendicular at the moment it crosses the meridian, a moon-like mirroring of the balancing agent of the "Scales of Justice".

This image was a foretelling of the coming of Christ, born out of *sacrifice* and remembered with the words, "*I lay down my life for the sheep.*"

Thus, it is not surprising to find the constellation of **Boötes**, the "Ploughman", leading the way into the *Air sign* of Libra. Bo meaning "coming" leads to Boötes, the *Coming One*. The great star **Arcturus,** whose name means the "Watcher" (or Guardian), is the main star of this constellation and stands at the threshold (29½°Virgo) leading into Libra, as a true Michaelic figure and guardian of the threshold. Here we are reminded of **Michael** who bears the Scales of Justice and was depicted in earlier times in the original zodiac as a standing figure holding the **Scales**, but since the time of Ptolemy has been forgotten.

The *heaped up* mid-point in the Libra sign thus becomes an image of the *altar* of Christ's *sacrifice* for humanity and the earth. The "upper" end of the beam of the scales of Libra is named "Zuben el Chamali", which means the "price that covers". This leads us to understand that the inner work of Libra is the great work of *atonement*, a work of the heart oriented to the *future*, bringing a personal and social idealism. This is the daily walk of meeting the *winds* (air) and constancy of *change* (future) with *equanimity*.

Crux – The Southern Cross
"The Vesica Piscis"

Just when Libra "reaches" her midpoint in her rise above the horizon in the southern hemisphere, there appears down below a most dazzling sight, the star configuration named "***Crux***" which is also called the "*Cross of Pardon*". This star configuration (mirroring the stars marking the beam and the balance pans of the scales in Libra) is a group of stars in the formation of a cross. The Italian navigator Amerigo Vespucci, who claimed to be the first European to see this configuration in 1501, called it the "***Mandorla***". Literally this means "almond shaped", describing the form of the vesica piscis reminding us of the pattern of light which we see surrounding images of the Virgin Mary.

In the gathering of research for these study materials, the discovery of "**Crux**" inspired such delight that only poetry could suffice:

This dazzling crown of colors so bright dance in the vesica piscis, the pattern that surrounds the bodies of saints and shines like a "Cross of Pardon".

When seen through a lens, this glorious sight becomes jewelry fit for a crown, a few strong reds with blues, greens and yellows in pale tinted color, more than half-drowned in radiant light.

Thus, the scales of justice are balanced just right by the grace of Christ's glorious deed symbolized by this cross in heaven. As a prize of great love and a witness to truth – the stars of the cross serve to balance the "Scales" forever.

Now the heavens at night sound the glory of Christ, and Sophia's robes do him justice. For the "Risen One" has set his own seal to speak for the pardon of man – with these stars called the "Cross of Pardon".

Now the deed is complete. Let there be no defeat, for this glorious cross shines in heaven.

And God sent a Queen that was fit for the crown to rule over the starfield called Libra, for Venus now measures the "Scales" with music and love, and decrees that each day be a treasure.[43]

Thus, the crown of beauty comes to balance the measure...

Enjoy the dance of Libra.

---

[43] Venus is considered the ruler of Libra.

Libra Meditation Work: *"Contentment becomes equanimity..."*

Sun in Libra: October 18 – November 17

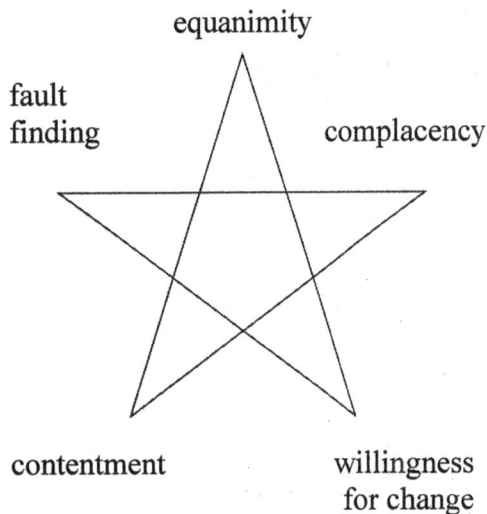

equanimity

fault
finding   complacency

contentment   willingness
                         for change

Sense of balance.

The Libran concerns of beauty, order and harmony can also be a source of great tension – bringing the question of how to "balance the measure"…

how to meet the challenge of discontent when things do not measure up to the scale of perfection?

The lower two points provide the foundation required to achieve the higher aspect of Libra. The lower left-hand corner is the virtue. The lower right-hand corner is what is needed along with the virtue in order to arrive at the uppermost point. The mid-points are what the lower points become if taken to extremes.

Virtue: Contentment – *"Blessed are the contented, for they shall have equanimity."*

This challenge which is met so beautifully in the perfection of our human form (as a given) must now be maintained both on the soul and spiritual level, in our daily walk through life.

Balanced thought, becomes balanced action, and a certain standard of uprightness which requires an alignment with higher consciousness.

In order to come into the measuring scale of true uprightness the image of securing a Christmas tree can be helpful. Without the balance from below which secures the trunk, the stability and vertical alignment of the tree are hopeless. Libra brings the challenge to maintain an equilibrium in our daily life so as not to lose our spiritual uprightness.

Libra Individuals
Sun in **Libra:** *"Worlds sustain worlds"*

Among the disciples, the archetypal representative of Libra was Thomas, the twin. Thomas, we remember, as doubting the wounds of the "Risen One". Thomas later went to India and was not present at the death and ascension of Mary.

It is through the life of Thomas, the disciple from which our expression "doubting Thomas" comes – describing the activity of weighing up in the seeking for truth and justice. In the process of "weighing up" doubt prevails until the truth is found. Then the doubt gives way to certainty.

Sun in **Libra** Individuals

first decan – Moon – Boötes (the Ploughman)
Emperor Augustus (1˚), French philosopher Henri Bergson (2˚), French social
philosopher Saint-Simon (3˚), German playwright Heinrich von Kleist (3˚), the French
poet Rimbaud (4˚), Swedish chemist and industrialist Alfred Nobel (5½˚), composers
Franz Liszt (5½˚) and Heinrich Schutz (6˚), English poet and philosopher Coleridge (7˚),
waltz composer Johann Strauss Jr. (9˚), Picasso (9½˚), Welsh poet Dylan Thomas (9½˚).

second decan – Saturn – Corona (Northern Crown) and Crux (Southern Cross)
English author Evelyn Waugh (10½˚), Neoplatonist Porphyry (11½˚), President Theodore
Roosevelt (11½˚), violinist Paganini (12½˚), poet Ezra Pound (14½˚), President Dwight
D. Eisenhower (15˚), Romantic poet John Keats (16˚), Florentine Platonist Marsilio
Ficino (18˚), architect Christopher Wren (18˚), French Queen Marie Antoinette (19˚).

third decan – Jupiter – Centaurus (the Centaur)
Russian revolutionary Trotsky (21˚), scientist Marie Curie (22˚), Roman poet Virgil
(23˚), Captain James Cook (23½˚), playwright Friedrich Schiller (26˚), novelist
Dostoevsky (26½˚), sculptor Rodin (28˚), Indian Prime Minister Nehru (29½˚) – all were
born when the Sun was in Libra.

Cosmic *Eurythmy*
"In the Image and Likeness…"

Antares

Scorpio – Intuition

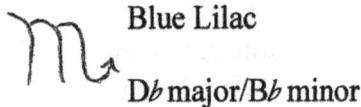

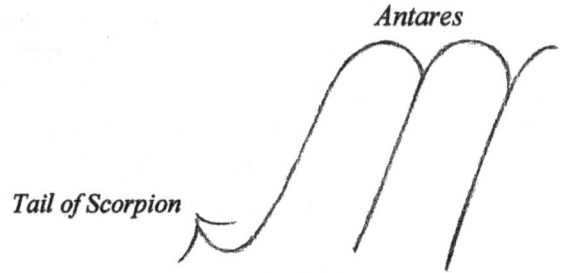

Blue Lilac

D♭ major/B♭ minor

Tail of Scorpion

With Scorpio, the streaming that was experienced from *within* in the Virgo gesture becomes an *outward* expression and is experienced as the serpentine spark of life that coils up the spine like the sap of a tree and spirals out into the arms like the branching of trees or wings caught in the wind.

These forces are the shaping streaming for the forming of the human reproductive and excretory organs, with a streaming around the brow and nose, centering in the larynx and throat.

In ancient times the constellation of Scorpio was imagined as an *Eagle*, soaring to the heights, where thinking (brow) becomes the power of seeing, making possible a fully conscious clairvoyance – the leap of intelligence toward *intuition*.

The Scorpio eurythmy form celebrates the serpentine flow of etheric streaming that weaves creatively between heaven and earth. With our arms we mirror the "S" *sound*, soaring toward the heights and then weaving back toward earth concluding with the Scorpio *gesture*. The gesture suggests the "sting of the Scorpion's tail" as intuition penetrates our earthly thinking. This is the mystery of the "sting of death" which creates the "bed of silence" necessary to *resurrection*, the birth of *intuition*.

We imagine ourselves surrounded by the color blue lilac *as we dance to music* written in the key of D♭ major. With the color blue lilac we can hold in consciousness how "*cosmic life forces work into the world of substance*".

In the cosmic *dance* of **Scorpio** the dancer becomes the *upright* staff of the *caduceus*, as the arms trace the pattern of the two entwined serpents – mirroring one another (left arm, forward "S"/ right arm, backward "S") – forming a figure "8" which crosses over at the heart and rises upward opening to the heights of the *Eagle* and then returns to the earth, retracing the figure "8" (*entwined "S" sounds*) while flowing down concluding with the Scorpion gesture (symbolizing the *sting* of the Scorpion).

We imagine ourselves in a mist of blue lilac light as we dance to music written in the key of D♭ major (the major key corresponding to Scorpio).

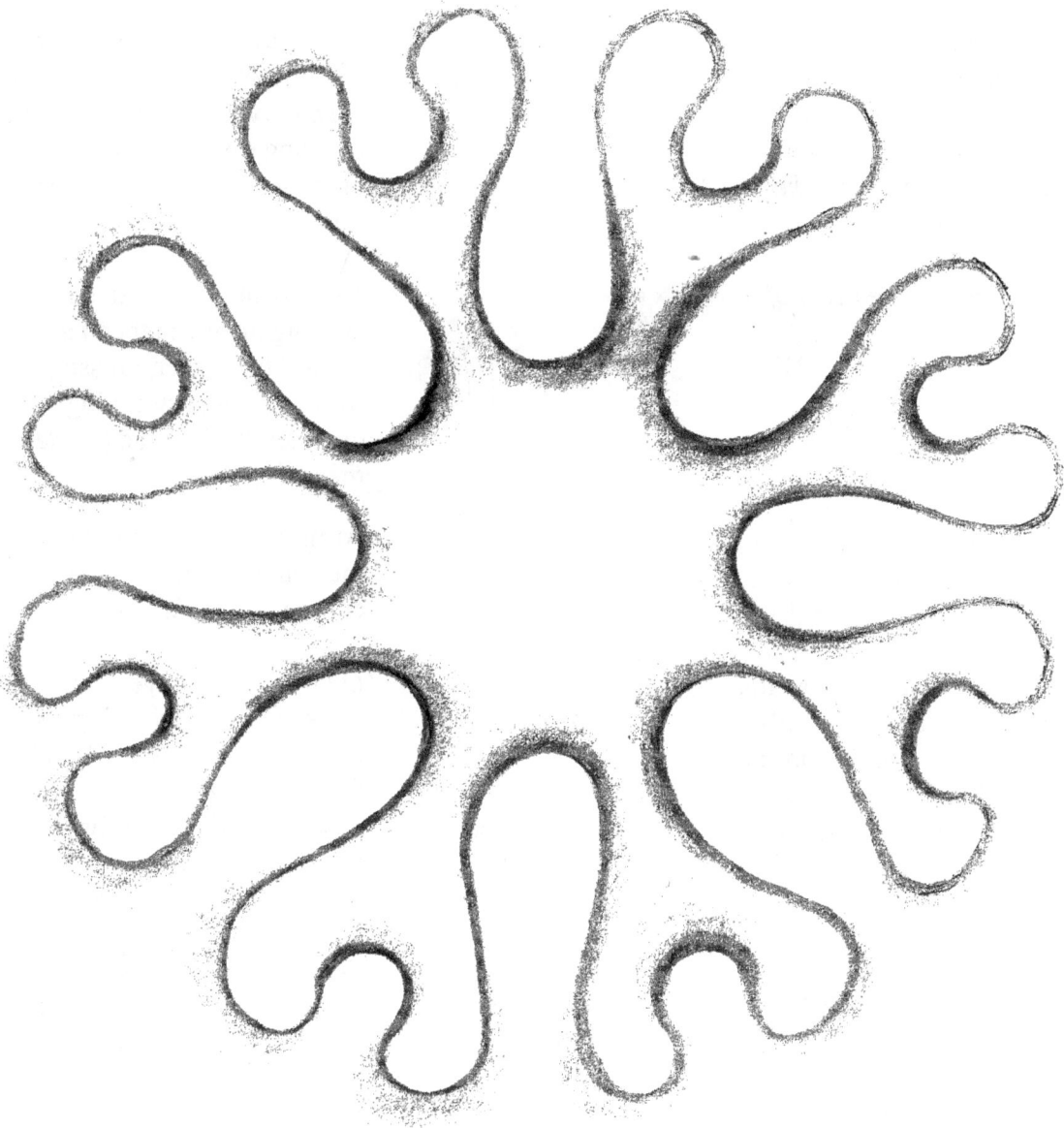

Scorpio Choreography

Cosmic Dance of Scorpio

"Ruling and controlling forces, penetrating to hidden depths."

Scorpio *Eurythmy* Form:
Move in a small curve backward to the left, forming the *claw of the Scorpion.*

Continue moving forward, moving first left then right in a larger curve, and then move around to the left to the *heart of the Scorpion.*

"Ruling and controlling forces"

Highest point: *the heart of the Scorpion.*

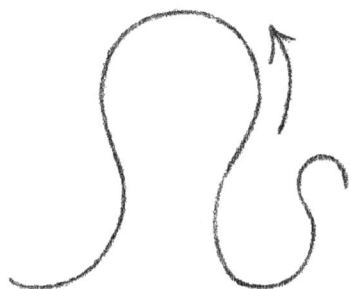

Curve backwards once again, first to the left, then slightly to the right and finally around to the left, curving forward in a small arc at the *Scorpion's tail.*

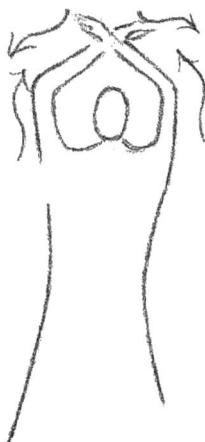

Pause at the midpoint of final curve, which is the tip of the Scorpion's tail. Stand with left foot slightly in front of right foot, *while forming Scorpio gesture.*

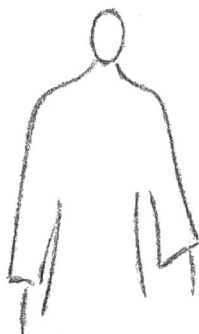

"penetrating to hidden depths."

Scorpio *Sound*: "S"
While forming the claw, begin the "S" sound gesture: open the arms at heart level, sweeping the arms together, cross the wrists at heart level and open arms *downwards.*

When arms are opened downward, draw them together in a slow curve sweeping upward, crossing over centrally, then open once again *moving arms upward.*

Arms continue to rise up, curving open and then back toward the center, crossing over again and sweeping open above the head (*eagle takes flight*).

Arms reach highest point at the center of large forward curve (*heart of the Scorpion*).

On backward movement, arms continue sweeping "S" curves as they lower. A small "S" gesture *ascending up and down* is made while forming the final curve, completing with *the Scorpio gesture.*

Scorpio *Gesture*: *At the midpoint of final curve,* stand erect, arms extended down at sides, palms facing in with… left arm extended out to left, palm open *fingers together* pointing down toward earth.

Scorpio – The Scorpion > Eagle > Dove   (November 17– December 17)
The mystery of death and resurrection

In ancient times the fixed stars in the region of Scorpio were beheld in the shape of an *Eagle*. Thus, the constellation of Scorpio bears within it both the sting of death which we associate with the image of the *Scorpion*, and the rising up of consciousness which we associate with the *Eagle*. These are the themes of death and resurrection.

This is the story foretold in the life of the "*Risen One*", the Christ mystery and the promise of the *Church* of John, which has the symbol of the *Eagle*. One of the four holy living creatures around the throne of God described by St. John in *The Revelation to John* is "like a flying eagle". This is the promise of the rising Sun and the transformative forces of enlightened thinking.

Scorpio brings the sting of death toward transformation, a call for the inner alchemy which requires the faculty of higher consciousness and insight.

It is said that the ancient alchemists taught that iron could be transformed into gold when the Sun was in the region of Scorpio. This is interesting because Scorpio is said to be the birthplace of *Mars*, the planet we associate with iron. The planet Mars is considered the *ruler* of Scorpio. Here the Mars influence is especially strong, bringing the quality of an "iron will", requiring an inner work of alchemy to *temper* and forge the "iron will" into pure gold.

The main star *Antares* (15°♏) is called the *rival* to Mars, due to the intensity of its red color which rivals the red planet Mars. Antares is the brightest star in the constellation and is referred to as the "*Heart of the Scorpion*". Here we can imagine the alchemist's fiery furnace as the fiery *feeling* heart. What greater power than the heart to transform consciousness. Antares is one of the Four Royal Stars marking the western arm of the cross, opposite Aldebaran (15° ♉) the "Eye of the Bull" in the East. As mentioned earlier, the "Royal Stars" bring us into connection with the "Royal Way", the path of *initiation* and *transformation*.

To understand the work of transformation initiated in the region of Scorpio, one can experience that here the struggle with *false pride* (set forward in Leo), and the *faculty of judgement* necessary for discernment (birthed from the womb of Virgo) are intensified as well as the qualities gained in the region of Cancer, of an evolved sense of feeling (*sense ability*) – each combine to create a feeling of *vulnerability*. The sting of the Scorpion can be quite deadly in the lower aspect of Scorpio, for this is the sting of self defense and protection.

Here the influence of **Mars** whose higher aspect is *Morality* and the speaking of *Truth*, can also deliver the *sting* of the wounding word (Mars rules the larynx and thus the faculty of speech). The Scorpion wounds in an effort to protect her extraordinary sense-ability. *Her work is to transform her feeling of vulnerability – and thus give freedom to her sense ability to serve others.*

The supporting role of **"The Starry Script"**
"A great eagle with great wings of diverse colors took the highest branch of the cedar."

If we look to the starry script for the answer to the riddle of the Scorpion/ Eagle/Dove imagination, we can observe that the *claws* of the Scorpion reach upward. The Scorpion's *claws* form the shape of a vessel or *holy grail* to receive the *Dove* of *Inspiration* and *Intuition*.

One way of forming an imagination of the higher aspect of **Scorpio**, "the *Eagle"*, is in terms of that which is set forward in the working of the *High Priestess*[44] *(*see *"Arcanum II"* in <u>Meditations On The Tarot)</u>, wherein the task is to become inwardly still and calm, foregoing the temptation to judge too quickly, to define or jump to conclusions. Thus, the reflective *waters* of insight (Scorpio is a *Water* sign) can present themselves in clarity bringing accurate intuitions to guide one's actions with temperance and wisdom. Here the destructive force of *pride* gives way to the strength of inner *sovereignty* and resolve.

If we expand our awareness out to the neighboring stars which support Scorpio, we find that beneath the *claws* of the Scorpion reside the stars which form the shape of **Lupus**, "the *Wolf*", which comes from the root word meaning *"victim of justice"*. Lupus is the slain victim of the *"sword of truth"* carried by the **Centaur**. In ancient times Lupus was also called *"Sura"*, meaning a sheep or lamb. For the Egyptians this was *Horus*, the beloved son of Osiris and Isis, while the Coptic name was *Harpocrates,* who was called the *"Silent One"*, also meaning *"Victim of Justice."*[45]

As we enter into the beginning regions of Scorpio [46] (a region which is said to be *ruled by Mars*), we see the image of the *Wolf*, which like the *claws* of the Scorpion might be experienced as an image of aggression and ferocity – having been *"stilled"* by the *"Sword of Truth"*. We can think of the wolf that was tamed by St. Francis or the she wolf that suckled the twins *Romulus* and *Remus*, the founders of Rome. The mystery name of Rome is Amor. Roma (*in ancient times associated with war and conquest)* when reversed becomes amor – meaning love.

We can experience in the story of **Lupus**, the *"sting of death"* brought by the Scorpion, as a *sacrifice*, a *"silencing"* of preconceived thought in order to come into an experience of *insight* (the Eagle) which can nourish and suckle the soul of humanity. Now, if we remember that Scorpio is thought to be a water sign, we can understand that the waters must be stilled in order to bring clear reflection.

This is a tremendous work on the part of the heart of Scorpio, a heroic effort for this central region (decan) which is *ruled* by the Sun and attended by the great Sun hero **Hercules**, whose stars support this region. Hercules, whose twelve labors symbolize the passage of the Sun through the Zodiac, treads the **Dragon** underfoot, whose head is marked by the star **Rastaban** (17°Scorpio).

---

[44] In astrological terms Scorpio is considered a feminine sign.

[45] A profound understanding of sacrifice is given in chapter V of <u>Meditations On The Tarot</u>.

[46] (0°♏) Start of Jesus' 40-day fast – an image of sacrifice and silencing; (1½ °♏) Judas Iscariot becomes a disciple; (2°♏) Conception of the Nathan Mary.

This is the work which is at the heart of Scorpio, *to tame the stinging tongue in order to reach for the higher truth of the Eagle and the Dove.*

In support of this challenge we see **Ophiucus**, the "*Serpent Holder*", blessing the good work of the Scorpion in the final region (decan) of Scorpio. This decan is *ruled by Mercury*, reminding us of the wisdom of the right use of poisons as the secret of medicine. We associate Mercury with the caduceus, the symbol of healing, which comprises an *upright* staff around which two serpents are entwined. This is an appropriate symbol for this region of the Scorpion's sting (3rd decan).

This calls for the sting of harsh judgment to be transformed into the work of compassion.

Scorpio Meditation Work – *"Patience becomes insight..."*

Sun in Scorpio: November 17 – December 17

"Patience is a necessary ingredient of genius" Disraeli.

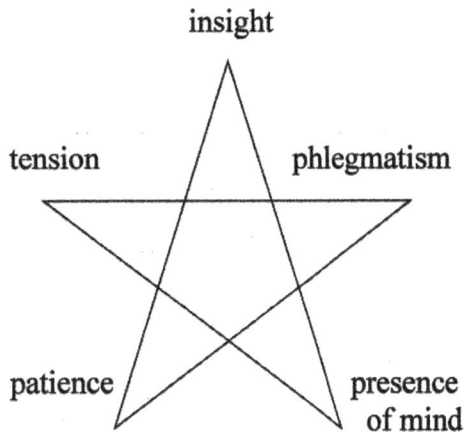

insight

tension   phlegmatism

patience   presence
                           of mind

Challenge is to temper the "sword of truth" with mercy.

Ability to pierce and conquer intellectually with the goal of insight...

to penetrate the hidden (occult) intentions (mystery).

The lower two points provide the foundation required to achieve the higher aspect of Scorpio. The lower left-hand corner is the virtue. The lower right-hand corner is what is needed along with the virtue in order to arrive at the uppermost point. The mid-points are what the lower points become if taken to extremes.

Virtue: Patience: *"Blessed are the patient for they shall receive insight."*
Sense: Smell

Exercise: To avoid the temptation of fighting for its own sake, or in the words of Manilius, that of *"not laying down arms, even in peace."* Work to soften the *"shell of self protection"* which leads to isolation and secrecy due to pride. Be aware of control of emotions, and extremes of sensitivity and introspection.

Scorpio Individuals
Sun in **Scorpio** – *"Existence consumes being."*

The greatest archetypal representatives of Scorpio are found within the circle of the twelve disciples with Judas representing the sting of death and Lazarus/John representing the Eagle or transformed illumined higher consciousness revealed in *The Revelation to John*.[47]

Other examples are: William Blake (Eagle) and Winston Churchill (Scorpion) both born with Sun conjunct *Antares* (15˚). The life of Churchhill, the great *warrior,* demonstrates the highest aspects of the "iron will" of *Mars* (Mars rules Scorpio), and the *courage* of the *heart (Antares)* to fight against evil for the good (Dove). In contrast, the life of William Blake, the great visionary, writer, poet, and painter demonstrates the highest aspects of transcendental thinking (Eagle/Dove).

---

[47] According to the spiritual research of Rudolf Steiner, Judas reincarnated as St. Augustine, having received the etheric body of Jesus Christ, a magnificent example of transformation.

Further examples of **Scorpio** individuals

first decan – Mars – Lupus (the Wolf – the Sacrifice)
Composer Paul Hindemith (1°), Roman Emperor Domition (1½°), Field Marshal
Montgomery (1½°), astronomer William Herschel (2°), Catholic philosopher Jacques
Maritain (3°), French mathematician d'Alembert (4°), composer Carl Maria von Weber
(5°), Swedish writer Selma Lagerlof (5½°), composer Benjamin Britten (6½°), General
Charles de Gaulle (6½°), French writer and philosopher Voltaire (9°), Martin Luther (9°),
painter Toulouse-Lautrec (9½°), industrialist and philanthropist Andrew Carnegie (10°),
Pope John XXIII (10°).

second decan – Sun – Hercules
Mathematician Theon of Alexandria (11°), philosopher Spinoza (13°), communist
theoretician Friedrich Engels (14½°), medical hypnotist Charcot (15°), Mark Twain (15°),
writer Bronson Alcott (15½°), King Charles I of England (19°), physicist Werner
Heisenberg (19°), poet Rainer Maria Rilke (19½°), St. Augustine (20°) is also an
outstanding example of the inspiration of Scorpio.

third decan – Mercury – Ophiucus (the Serpent Bearer)
Writer Thomas Carlyle (21°), Finnish composer Jean Sibelius (24°), Russian writer
Alexander Solzhenitsyn (25°), French composer Caesar Franck (25½°), Roman Emperors
Tiberius (25½°) and Vespasian (27°), composer Hector Berlioz (27°), writer Jonathan
Swift (28½°), French novelist Gustave Flaubert (28½°).

Nunki

Sagittarius Taking aim

Rose Lilac *"The breath of the etheric"*

A♭ major / F minor

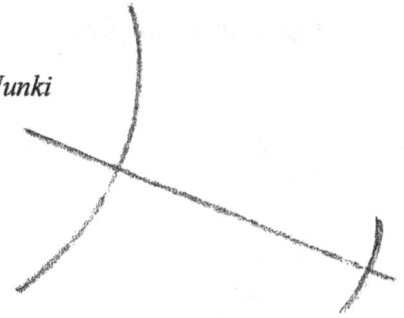

If we follow with our eyes across to the left of *Antares*, the "Heart of the Scorpion", we come to the constellation of Sagittarius. The etheric streaming in the region of the starry heavens known as **Sagittarius** flows in the form of an *arrow* aimed from a *bow*.

Thus, the naming of Sagittarius comes from the root word, "*Sagitta*", which in Latin means *arrow*. The ancient clairvoyants envisaged the stars which gathered in the starfield of Sagittarius as "the *Archer*", a centaur holding a bow armed with an arrow pointing toward the tail of the Scorpion.

The centaur, we recall from the story of the celestial **Centaur** beneath Libra, is "half man, half animal", a condition which describes the process of *transformation*. As the archetypal form for the *human being* comes from the constellations, it is the *upright being* of the *Archer,* who *leads* the horse and *aims* the arrow, who participates in the shaping of the human being.

The shaping forces from the realm of Sagittarius are the *guiding* forces of the horseman, the thighs and upper arms, also the forebrain with the central point at mid brow. With this understanding, we can experience the Archer taking *aim* by finding a central focus.

It is said that the central focus of Sagittarius is to *know* the truth. Thus, the eurythmy gesture "G" uses the force of the upper arms to push away the forces of darkness, to open the veiled secrets and the curtains of deception, with an *aim* to reveal the light of clarity and to understand the truth.

The eurythmy gesture for Sagittarius gives expression to the Archer taking aim with this single minded purpose. As the Archer takes aim, the upper arms and the thighs hold the tension of the *guiding* principle necessary for a steady aim.

As we dance the cosmic dance of Sagittarius, we imagine ourselves surrounded by the color Rose Lilac as we move to music in the key of A♭ major or F minor.

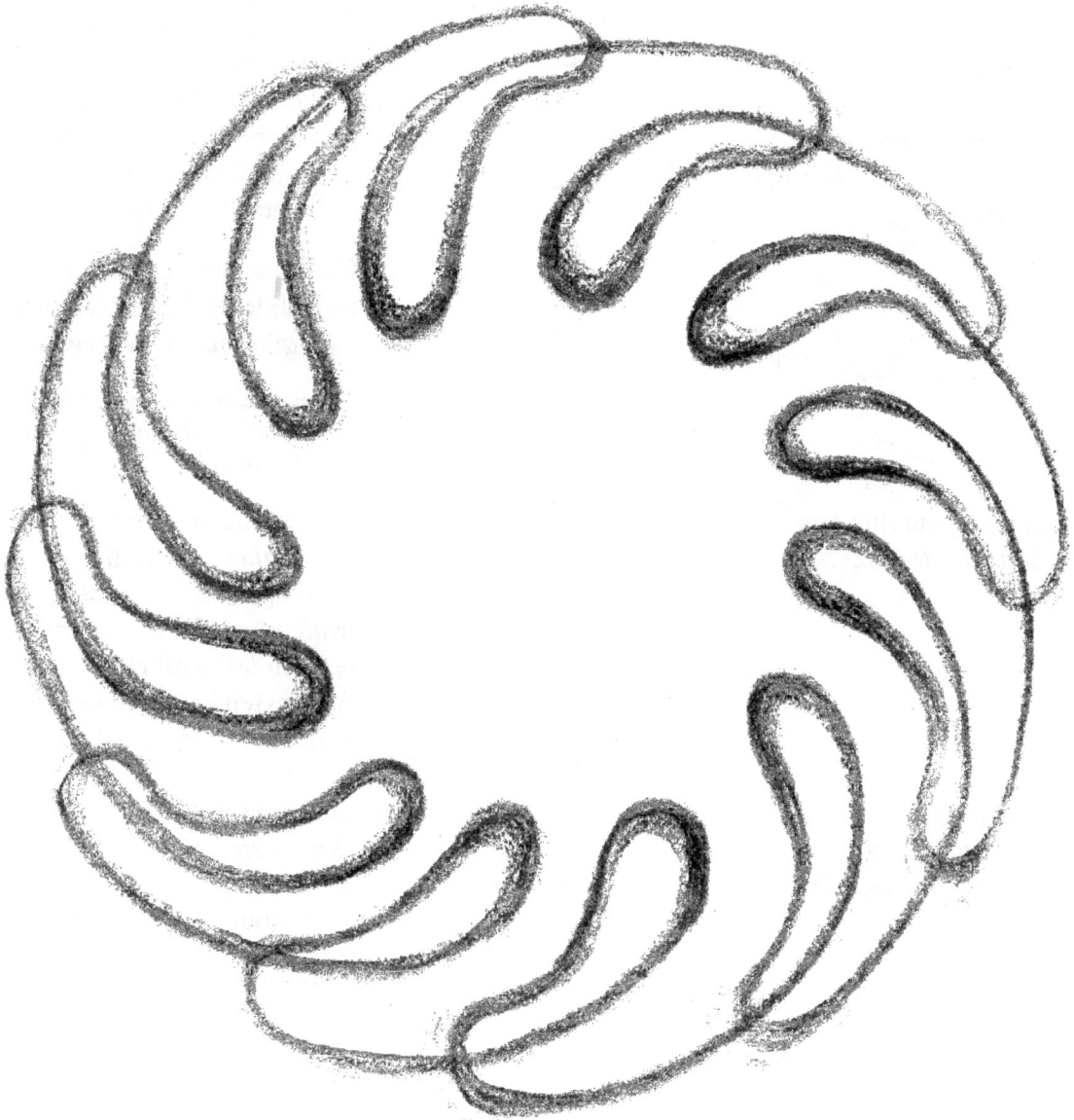

Sagittarius Choreography

Sagittarius Cosmic Dance Form
"Drawing forth the light of clarity."

Sagittarius *eurythmy* form:
Begin moving back slightly to the right *with the first "G" sound.*

Retreating into silence in order to draw forth the light of clarity.

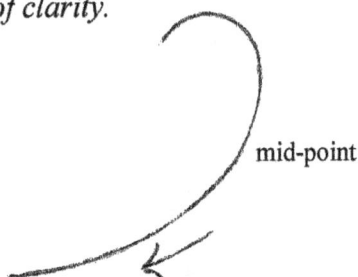

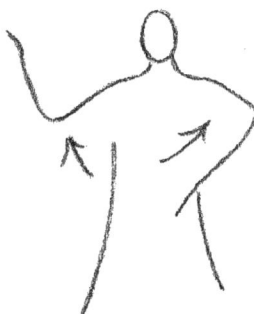

mid-point

Continuing curving around to the left *with the second "G" sound.*

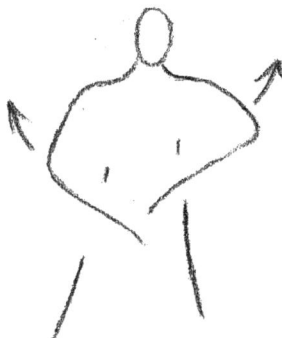

Now curve forward to right, stopping at mid-point of inner curve, *to form Sagittarius gesture.*

Sagittarius *sound*: "G":
While moving back, curving to the right, raise arms with elbows pointing out, hands centered heart level *right arm slightly higher than left, palms facing out away from body.* Push arms apart diagonally, *R. arm ascending and L. arm descending,* feeling resistance in upper arms, as though pushing aside heavy curtains.

Continue until elbows are fully extended apart (*elbows bent at about 90 degrees*).

Having reached the outer curve, draw arms together again at heart level for the second "G" sound

reverse the arm gesture (left arm *higher* than right arm), pushing arms/forearms apart *while moving left;* continue *moving left* until elbows are fully extended (*elbows bent at about 90 degrees*).

Sagittarius *gesture*:
(*Knees sink slightly until tension is felt in thighs*). Right foot forward, left back. Body upright as though upright in a saddle (weight *balanced* between *backward* left and *forward* right knee).

Right arm raised with fist lightly clenched (*at heart region*), elbow pointing forward. *Press* right fist *into elbow socket of left arm.* Bring left hand forward to enclose right elbow. Press right forearm against left forearm.

Sagittarius *"The Archer"* (December 17 – January 15)

The centaur's half human, half horse form suggests the halfway point of the human being's triumph, and/or taming of the animal nature in order to come into the fullness of true humanity – to experience what it means to be truly human.

The region of Sagittarius is considered related to the quality of fire, and its nature is considered to be changeable or *mutable*. Here we experience the force of "dynamic tension" which recalls the point of transition that we see in the image of the centaur.

In legend, the most famous centaur was the Greek hero **Chiron**, who was very wise. It is said that it was Chiron, the great teacher and healer, who taught Jason and the Argonauts who set sail in the ship Argo in search of the "golden fleece".

The wisdom of Chiron is the gift of **Jupiter** the "Great Beneficent" or "Great Cosmic Thinker". Jupiter is at *home* in Sagittarius. Thus, when Jupiter is in Sagittarius, it manifests considerable strength and influence – indeed the full flavoring of its character.

Galactic Center (2° ♐)
The most evolved Sagittarian teacher and healer of all time was Jesus Christ whose birth star **Nunki**[49] is located at the shaft of the Archer's arrow, which points directly toward the *Galactic Center*[50] (2° Sagittarius). This is an astronomical finding that has only recently been discovered. Through *Nunki* (17½° ♐), the birth star of Jesus Christ, we can know that the "*aim*" of Sagittarius is toward the future transformation of both the earth and humanity. This is the work of the Cosmic Christ to bring humankind and the earth into connection with the heart of God (Galactic Center).

The life and miracles of Jesus Christ perfectly portray this connection with the *Galactic Center*, the fiery realm of the "Father". In Christian tradition the realm of the Seraphim, *depicted in art with wings of fire and whose movements deliver the flames of "pure love"*, reaches up to receive the fire of Divine Love emanating from the realm of the Father.

The need to *know the truth* and to *understand* is said to be the most central aspect or cause for the Sagittarian nature or character. Thus, we can imagine the "dynamic tension" of the Archer's *aim* drawing forth *understanding* from the *Galactic Center*, the Ultimate Source, the realm of the Father (also referred to as the "*Great Central Sun*"), a *source* of understanding grounded in *pure love*.

Beethoven was born when the Sun was conjunct with the Galactic Center (2° Sagittarius). We can imagine him as *Prometheus* stealing the transformative, creative fire from heaven, drawing it down into his music through the "dynamic tension" of the Archer's bow.

---

[49] Research of Robert Powell indicates Nunki to be the bright star closest to the Sun at the birth of Jesus.
[50] All the stars in the heavens, including our Sun, revolve around the Galactic Center, which thus represents the Ultimate Source of all existence.

The great German mathematician and astronomer Kepler was born when the Sun was near the flanks of the centaur, calling forth the power of tremendous will forces to calculate and to penetrate through, with the Archer's single minded "*aim*", into the mysteries of the universe. This is a fine example of the "dynamic tension" that seeks to understand.

The challenge provoked by this region and source of "dynamic tension" in Sagittarius is the necessity to control or *temper* one's words or actions. This comes to expression with the Archer's aim (arrow) pointed toward the tail of the Scorpion. In the eagerness for truth, Sagittarius can inspire a certain forthrightness in speech that can be biting and wounding, experienced as an arrow aimed through the strong will forces of the centaur.

Here we see the challenge of Sagittarius is to tame the animal force of the tongue and endeavor toward the higher choices of developed consciousness.

A myth (legend) helpful for an understanding of the challenges presented through the qualities inspired in the region of Sagittarius is the story of Zeus (Jupiter), the son of Chronos (Saturn). Rhea, the wife of Chronos, hid Jupiter in a cave to protect him from Saturn. Through growing up in a cave (*inner reflection),* Jupiter developed the faculties of higher consciousness. This was Jupiter's destiny to become the "Great Cosmic Thinker." And, as mentioned earlier, Jupiter is the *ruler* of Sagittarius.

Sagittarius requires a "*reining in*" of the instincts and a *tempering* of the temptation toward the *sanguine* pursuit of multiplicity in order to deepen the understanding for higher truths.

In the legend of Jupiter's confinement, it is said that an *eagle* provided the *nectar* of nourishment (*higher truth*) for the development of Jupiter's higher faculties. (The eagle represents the realized mastery of the higher faculties developed in Scorpio.) This is the promise that is held out to all those who exert themselves to exercise their higher faculties of thought. The reward offered by Jupiter is the nectar of divine truth.

There is a strong resonance between the higher qualities of Sagittarius of *intuition* and *idealism,* which find themselves mirrored again in the higher qualities of Jupiter.

Again, if we expand our awareness out to the starry script which surrounds Sagittarius, we find in the myths and legends a deepening for our understanding of the work of the heavens supporting this region.

The Starry Script

In the region of the Galactic center (2° ♐), the fiery heart of the great Central Sun, we see **Ara**, *The Altar*, which means "*Burning Pyre*". This is a decan *ruled by Venus,* bringing a quality of worship and devotion to fan the flames of *pure love* that pulse from this region of the *Galactic Center,* which is the single minded "aim" and purpose of the Archer's arrow. We can think of Moses and the burning bush – Moses, the prophet whose tongue was tempered by pure love, and also Jesus' *Sermon on the Mount* which took place when the Sun (7½° ♐) was in alignment with the heart of God, in this first decan of Sagittarius.

In the central decan of Sagittarius we find the *Southern Crown* (**Corona Australis**). This is the crown of *birth* symbolized by the Sun's location at the birth of Jesus (16° ♐) in the heart of Sagittarius, an event which is remembered by the <u>Moon</u> which *rules* this region. Note the polarity with the *Northern Cross* in the central region of Libra where the <u>Full Moon</u> marked the *death* (*crucifixion*) of Jesus. Is this crown at the feet of the Archer an image of the "*signet of perfection, full of wisdom*" (<u>Ezekiel</u> 28:11) cast down? We are reminded here of the Grail theme of the precious stone that fell from the crown of Lucifer. "*How you are fallen from heaven, O day star, Sun of dawn*" (<u>Isaiah</u> 14:12).

In the final decan of Sagittarius we see **Lyra,** *the Lyre*, the instrument whose melodies when played by *Orpheus* tamed the wild beasts, and for which all of nature, rocks and trees, moved in order to listen. The Dragon guarding the "golden fleece" was put to sleep, and all beings, even the underworld, paid homage to Orpheus on account of his music.
Thus, *the Lyre* comes as support to the *will* of the Archer to tame the animal forces, in the service of the Divine through the power of music and the word.

The great star *Vega* (20½° ♐) in the constellation of the Lyre is close to the Solar Apex. This is the direction in which our Sun is moving within the local group of stars – the local movement of our Sun, seen in relation to the neighboring stars of our surrounding cosmos, is towards Vega.

Sagittarius Meditation Work: *"Control of tongue becomes feeling for truth..."*

Sun in Sagittarius: December 17 – January 15

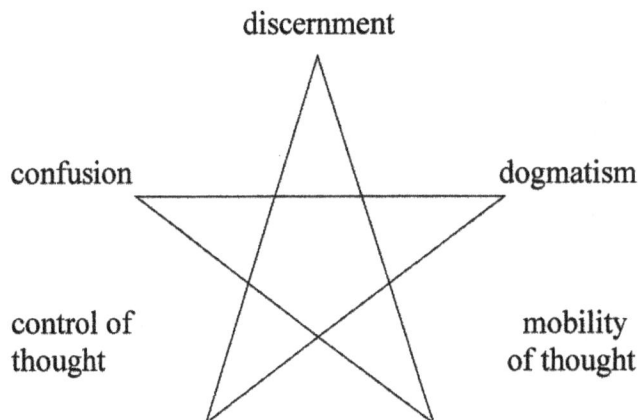

discernment

confusion   dogmatism

control of   mobility
thought   of thought

The lower two points provide the foundation required to achieve the higher aspect of Sagittarius. The lower left-hand corner is the virtue. The lower right-hand corner is what is needed along with the virtue in order to arrive at the uppermost point. The mid-points are what the lower points become if taken to extremes.

Virtue: Self discipline – *"Blessed are the self disciplined, for they shall know the truth."*
Sense: Taste
Exercise: Control of animal nature.

The image of the Archer is sometimes depicted as looking backwards. In the questing for truth it can be that one seeks retreat into the past for review and reconciliation with that which is already known.

However, the truth that serves the future is not found in retreat but rather in expansion. This we can experience with the eurythmy sound "G" to clear away, becoming inwardly firm. Thus, the outward exuberance (expansion) inspired in the region of Sagittarius is seeking to cultivate the inner activity of *opening* closed doorways to perception in order to deepen and expand the limitations of ordinary consciousness.

Sagittarius Individuals
Sun in **Sagittarius** – *"Growth attains power of existence."*

Jesus of Nazareth (16°), Kepler (26½°) and Beethoven (3°), are outstanding examples of Sagittarius. However, we can understand from the life of Nero, the Emperor of the Roman Empire from AD 54–68, a contrasting side of Sagittarius.

Nero (25°) is an example of the fiery nature of the strong will forces of Sagittarius backfiring, literally turning in upon the human being. We can recall that Nero, through an act of madness, set fire to the city of Rome. Nero was said to have forced his initiation into the spiritual mysteries before he was spiritually ripe, and this caused a backfiring of the "fire initiation trial" which brought about Nero's spiritual madness.

Further examples of **Sagittarius** individuals

first decan – Venus – Ara (the Altar)
Poet Heinrich Heine (0°), French physicist Henri Becquerel (1°), Russian painter Kandinsky (1½°), German Chancellor Willy Brandt (2½°), artist Paul Klee (3°), writer Jane Austen (3½°), British chemist Humphrey Davy (4°), Stalin (6°), Mary Queen of Scots (7°), British Prime Minister Benjamin Disraeli (7°), English poet John Milton (8½°), Mormon Joseph Smith (8½°), French playwright Jean Racine (10°).

second decan – Moon – Corona Australis (the Southern Crown)
Pope Leo X (11°), "Angel of the Battlefield" Clara Barton (11½°), writer Henry Miller (11½°), French bacteriologist Louis Pasteur (12½°), King Henri IV of France (13½°), Danish astronomer Tycho Brahe (13½°), visionary Nostradamus (14°), President Woodrow Wilson (15°), British Prime Minister William Gladstone (15°), writer Rudyard Kipling (16°), artist Henri Matisse (17°), Roman poet Horace (19°), St. Therese of Lisieux (20°).

third decan – Saturn – Lyra (the Lyre)
German Chancellor Konrad Adenauer (21½°), yoga teacher Yogananda (22½°), Russian composer Scriabin (22½°), Jakob Grimm (Grimm's Fairy Tales) (23°), archeologist Heinrich Schliemann (23½°), mathematician and astronomer Isaac Newton (24°), French writer Simone de Beauvoir (24°), President Richard Nixon (26°), Emperor Frederick II (28°), psychologist and philosopher William James (28½°), German poet Annette von Droste-Hulshoff (29°).

Cosmic *Eurythmy*
"In the Image and Likeness..."

Capricorn   Striving (pressing forward)

Peach Blossom *"the living image of the soul"*

E♭ major / C minor   *Deneb Algedi*

After passing through the realm of Sagittarius acquiring the dynamic tension of our *limbs*, our taking *"aim"* with our true spiritual task (*the overcoming of the lower animal will forces*) and becoming fully *upright* with *the Archer*, the region of ***Capricorn*** now provides the etheric shaping force for our knees and elbows, our eyes, and the entire skeletal structure, including our column of uprightness which culminates in the central form of the crown.

The horns of the ***Goat*** celebrate the gift of a fully *activated crown*. Much like the mountain goat, we become *able* and agile to climb the most precipitous levels of consciousness. The goat has overcome the sensuous appetites of Sagittarius and by becoming inwardly firm and upright is ready to set about the work of extracting nourishment from the most arid of landscapes.

Having acquired the *forebrain* and activated the *brow center*, Capricorn now works to *transform* the darkness into light – steady and ready to meet resistance from the rigid thought forms of the past. We give expression to the purpose of Capricorn with the Capricorn gesture.

With our left hand (heart side) held firmly (with closed palm) above the awakened forebrain (concentrating the etheric streaming into this center), we grasp our power of concentration – while the right hand (with palm open activating a streaming out of etheric force) extends forward to push through the preconceived thought patterns of the past, pressing diligently onward into the ever expanding thought patterns of the future.

As we dance the Capricorn form which traces the etheric flowing through the constellation, we imagine ourselves moving in the soft etheric light of peach blossom – experiencing the *blossoming* promise of initiatory soul activity. We dance to the music of the sounding key of Capricorn.

From the standpoint of inner firmness, we can now "taste" mobility, the gift of our structure. With the gift of mobility we can live and breathe and work in the current of change called the future – this we experience with the eurythmy sound "L", a flowing fountain of etheric movement.

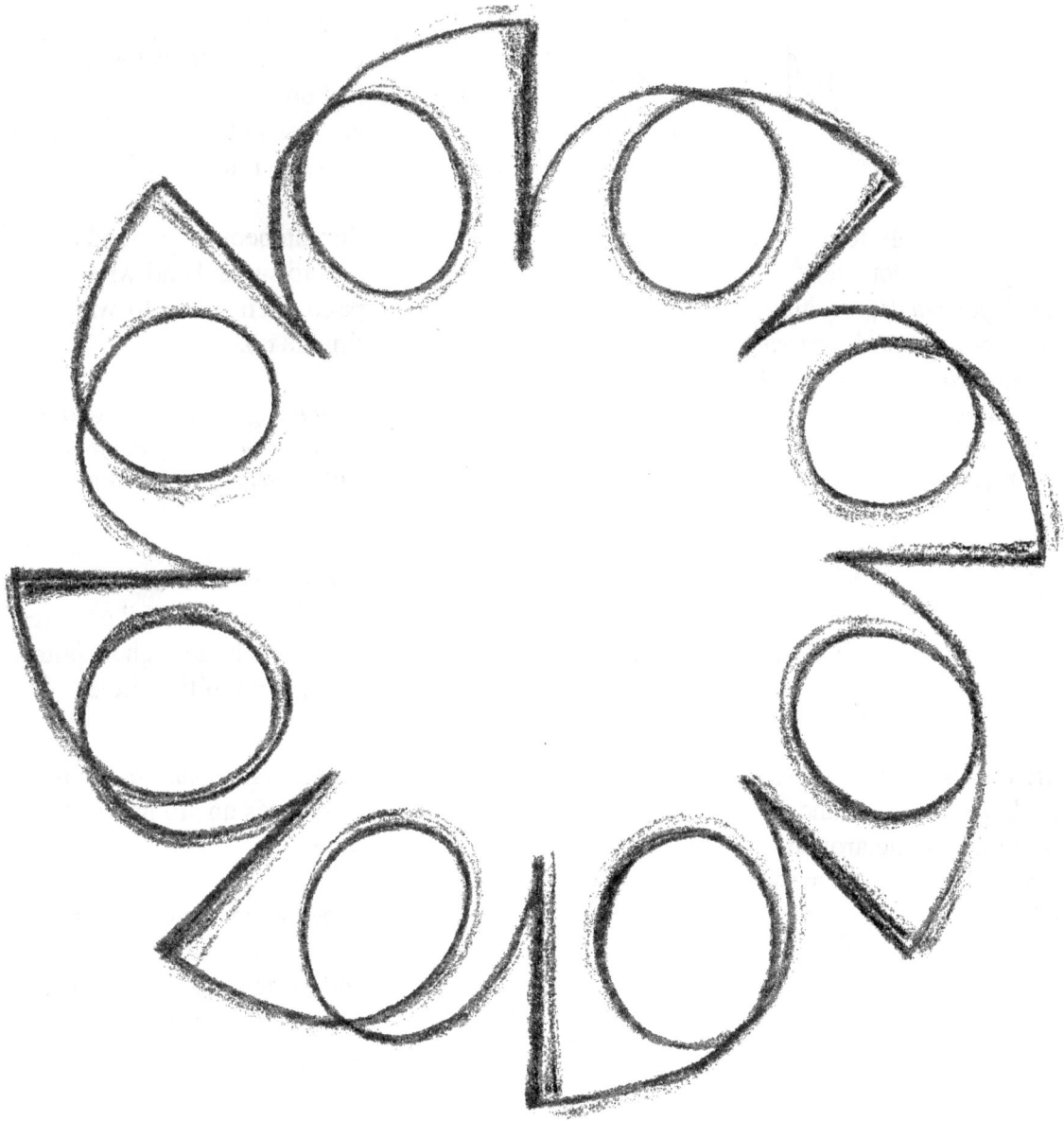

Capricorn Choreography

Capricorn Cosmic Dance Form
"Transforming darkness into light"

Capricorn *eurythmy* form:
At the horns of the Goat:
Take three steps forward, beginning with right foot, *while forming Capricorn gesture.*

Pause, with right foot forward; left foot back, *weight forward*, pressing right knee forward, *pressing forward courageously with new ideas.*

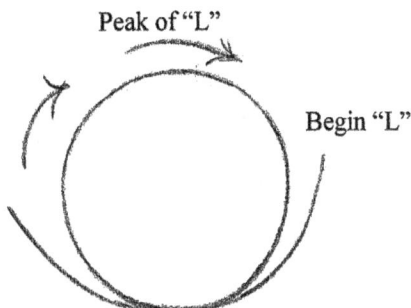

Peak of "L"

Begin "L"

Circle back to the left in a *clockwise* direction and continue circling around moving forward and to the left.

Complete the "L" while circling back and around to the left.

Capricorn *gesture*:
While stepping forward, slowly form Capricorn gesture...

Left arm with hand *lightly clenched* moves out to left side up above head and comes down from behind to rest on forehead. Bend hand at wrist so that knuckles point down to mid-brow line.

Simultaneously, extend right arm forward, bend wrist, palm open facing forward, fingers up.

In thinking (higher thought) one opens to the flow of the future while meeting the resistance of the past.

Capricorn *sound*: "L"
Slowly form the "L" gesture: Arms reach the highest point at the front of the circle.

With palms open, facing up, raise arms up along mid-line of body.

When hands reach above crown, turn the palms over and bring arms out and down in a flowing movement, *like a fountain.*

A flowing fountain of etheric movement, transforming darkness into light.

Capricorn – The Sea Goat   (January 15 – February 14)

The Capricorn sound "L" in eurythmy is a *water* sound describing the etheric waters of life, suggesting fluidity or flow. So too the formation of the human knees, elbow and the vertebrae suggest a certain mobility, the ability to turn or bend in order to bring about *change*.

These two ideas tell the story of Capricorn, for the region of the heavens which is known as the **Goat** was in ancient times seen as the **Sea-Goat**, a goat with a fishes' tail, evidence that a *change* has taken place in this region of Capricorn.

Here we have yet another foretelling of the promise of *transformation*. The region of the heavens where the etheric forces flow in the form of a fishes' tail is called the "watery region" (hence the fishes' tail). Correspondingly, this also foretells the process of metamorphosis that must take place in order to make way for the region of Aquarius and the Waterman's promise of the coming of the Etheric Christ.

Interestingly, the planet **Mars** is *exalted* in this watery region at the tailend of Capricorn (28° ♑). Mars is associated with the *courage* to move toward change. Thus, Mars can help to move humanity and the Earth through this time of great change toward the future of evolution.

Here we can imagine the work of the frugal Goat, who is able to subsist on the most arid of landscapes, capable and agile, able to make amazing leaps and tread gracefully over the most dangerous precipices. This tells the story of the process of higher thinking. The bone hard substance of the Goat's head forces (representing rigid thinking, grounded in the past) must give way and dissolve into the ability to swim, to be *fluid*, to be able to think *with* the *living currents* of the *future*. The goat's horns are essentially antennae for connecting to cosmic thought.

The Starry Script
If we read the starry script of the heavens we discover yet another story which can help us understand this process.

The region of the heavens where the cosmic etheric forces flow to shape the *head* of the Goat is home to a grouping of stars called "**Sagitta**", the *Heavenly Arrow*.
Ancient myth tells us, that the heavenly arrow is sent to *wound* the head forces making us ready to receive the wisdom of the cosmos, a sacrifice of the old in order to birth the new.

Sagitta is associated with the central decan (heart region) of Capricorn, and it is interesting to note that the Sun was in the middle of Capricorn (14½° ♑) when the *beheading of John the Baptist* took place, the archetypal story of the *sacrifice* of the head forces, which leads to *transformation*. According to Rudolf Steiner the forces of John the Baptist were given over to the risen *Lazarus*. Could it be that the early loss of life for John the Baptist also extended the life of Lazarus? Was it this sacrifice that made it possible for Lazarus to receive the writings of the Apocalypse on the island of Patmos at the age of 95 years and later (approaching 100 years of age) to write the Gospel of St. John? (*Lazarus wrote under the name John*).

A *Royal* Tale – *related to kings…*

6° Capricorn in the region of the horns of the Goat marks the Sun's location at the time of the *"Adoration of the Magi",* the visit of the three kings who welcomed the arrival of the new born Solomon Jesus, whose birth is described in the <u>Gospel of St. Matthew</u>.

The Egyptians especially celebrated the arrival of ten significant stars during the course of the year. They referred to these stars as the ten kings. ***Deneb Algedi***, which marks the tail of the Goat, was one of these stars – located at 28½°; it denotes the place of exaltation of Mars.

Clearly, the *royal way* to the *future* calls for *transformation.* Let us not allow *"our bread to become stone"* lest the *grace filled waters* of the etheric Christ not be able to *move* us forward to the *future.*

Saturn, the planet of cosmic memory – said to be attuned to the pattern of the past inscribed in the *akashic records* – is the *ruler* of Capricorn. This means that Capricorn is a region of the heavens where Saturn's forces are especially strong. Saturn's *kingly* task is given fertile ground in Capricorn, as Capricorn is considered the "gateway for the soul's return back to the spiritual world after death". Thus, one can sense how the constellation of Capricorn bears a strong impulse toward the *fulfillment* of karmic intention.[50] Capricorn encourages one to hold to one's karmic task (*spiritual covenant*), which ultimately entails nothing less than transformation. This is the path of the kings, the "Royal Way", the path of initiation.

Starry Script continued

We find **Aquila**, *the Eagle*, associated with the beginning region (first decan) of Capricorn. The Eagle corresponds to the *fully developed crown*, which is the promise of the horns of the goat. It was the eagle that brought nectar to Jupiter, who lay concealed in a cave by reason of the fury of Chronos (Saturn). *"I bore you on eagles' wings"* (<u>Exodus</u> 19: 4). And true it is that this first decan of Capricorn is *ruled by **Jupiter***.

According to legend the eagle guides the souls of the dead. Capricorn is considered the *"gateway to the afterlife"* or the *"gateway to the Sun"*. We see in the image of *Aquila,* the *wounded falling Eagle*, the symbol for the death of ordinary intelligence, making divine intelligence accessible.

This wounding is said to take place through the work of ***Sagitta***, *the Arrow*, which brings the *living word* of the Logos (*cosmic thinking*) to the central region of Capricorn, which correspondingly is *ruled by **Mars***, whose higher aspect is connected to bringing truth and morality to speech.

"Their arrows have sunk into me…I am utterly bowed down and prostrate" (<u>Psalms</u> *38:2,6*) This is the central decan of Capricorn, in which we find the knees (*change)* of the Goat, giving the capability of kneeling ("bowed down").

---

[50] After the mastery of the "reining in" of animality (Sagittarius), Saturn makes sure we hold to the promise of destiny in Capricorn.

And finally, in connection with the last decan of Capricorn, we see **Delphinus**, *The Dolphin*, joyfully celebrating this transformation of thought life in the watery region of the Goat-fishes' tail.

The Dolphin, like the "L" sound of Capricorn, is seen full of life, leaping like a fountain of *living water*. The Dolphin, which is sacred to *Apollo*, the Sun God, graces this region of the third decan which is *ruled* by the Sun.

Capricorn Meditation Work: *"Courage becomes the power of redemption..."*

Sun in Capricorn: January 15 – February 14

Courage is associated with Mars, which is exalted in Capricorn. And the influence of Saturn, the ruler of Capricorn, helps...

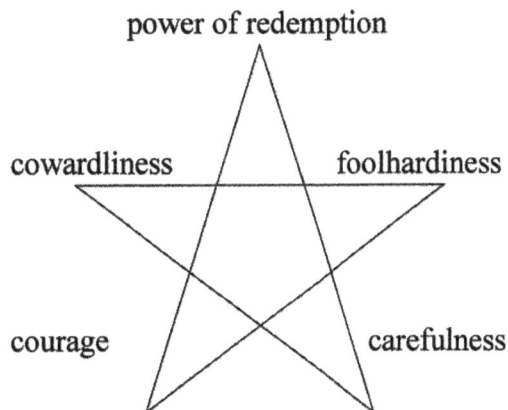

power of redemption

cowardliness   foolhardiness

courage   carefulness

to develop *conscience* – the insight to...

know what is right.

There is sometimes a tendency toward the ascetic Saturnine influence.

The lower two points provide the foundation required to achieve the higher aspect of Capricorn. The lower left-hand corner is the virtue. The lower right-hand corner is what is needed along with the virtue in order to arrive at the uppermost point. The mid-points are what the lower points become if taken to extremes.

Virtue: Courage
Sense: Sight
World View: Spiritism

Ideal: *"Blessed are the courageous for they shall have the power to redeem."*

Capricorn Individuals
Sun in **Capricorn**: *"May the future rest upon the past."*

first decan – Jupiter – Aquila (the Eagle)
Swiss educationist Pestalozzi (1˚), Martin Luther King (1½˚), Albert Schweitzer (1½˚), Swiss religious reformer Zwingli (2˚), British Prime Minister Lloyd George (4˚), French poet and playwright Molière (5½˚), artist Paul Cezanne (6˚), Benjamin Franklin (6½˚), writer Edgar Allen Poe (7˚), English engineer and inventor James Watt (8˚), Joan of Arc (8˚), Swedish playwright August Strindberg (9½˚).

second decan – Mars – Sagitta (the Arrow)
Romantic poet Lord Byron (10½˚),writer George Orwell (11˚), French electrical physicist Ampere (11˚), German writer Lessing (11½˚), English writers Somerset Maugham (12˚) and Virginia Woolf (12½˚), German writer and composer E. T. A. Hoffman (12½˚), King Friedrich the Great of Prussia (13˚), Scottish writer Robert Burns (13½˚), English writer Lewis Carroll (14˚), Roman orator and writer Cicero (15˚), German philosopher Schelling (15½˚), Russian philosopher Soloviev (16˚), Russian playwright Anton Chekhov (16˚), composer Mozart (16˚), explorer Henry Morton Stanley (16½˚), President Franklin Roosevelt (18˚), writer James Joyce (20˚), French philosopher Simone Weil (20˚).

Capricorn Individuals

third decan–Sun – Delphinus (the Dolphin)

Composer Franz Schubert (20½°), German theologian and resistance fighter Dietrich Bonhoeffer (21½°), composer Felix Mendelssohn (22°), President Ronald Reagan (23°), English science philosopher Francis Bacon (24°), psychologist Alfred Adler (25°), novelist Charles Dickens (25½°), artist Franz Marc (26°), science fiction writer Jules Verne (26½°), Jewish philosopher and theologian Martin Buber (26½°), German playwright Bertolt Brecht (28°), composer Alban Berg (28°), Swedish scientist and mystic Swedenborg (29°).

Cosmic *Eurythmy*
"In the Image and Likeness..."

Aquarius - To Know

Rose pink *"Feeling the source of all life"*

B♭ major / G minor

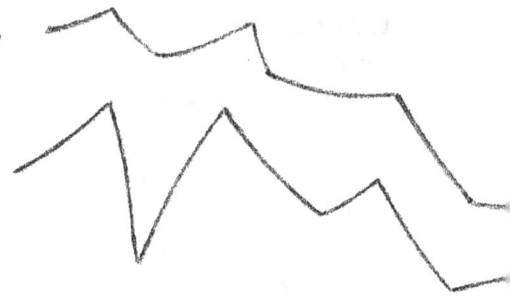

Whereas the Goat's path may feel like swimming "up stream" against the currents of the past, Aquarius brings freer waters. Having gained our sense of *spiritual sight* in order to know what is right in the region of Capricorn, the waters of Aquarius lead beyond the constraints and restraining forces which hold us to our promise of destiny.

The *healing of the paralyzed man at the pool of Bethesda* which took place when the Sun had just entered Aquarius (0½° ♒) gives an archetypal picture of the freedom born in the Aquarian waters.

These are the birthing waters of invention. Having to do with the element of Air, Aquarius is an Air sign, free of the boundaries of constraint. With Aquarius there comes a unique sense of freedom and warmth.

This region of the heavens known as Aquarius forms the archtypal pattern for our calves and forearms, as well as bringing a harmonization of all the centers.

The eurythmy form for Aquarius celebrates this coming together of harmonization and freedom – flowing in a lemniscatory pattern backwards (past) and forwards (future), weaving in and out in an ebb and flow movement. Gathering the fullness of past and future, we move ever onward towards new beginnings.

Aquarius is called the "Waterbearer" or "Waterman" because the stars that gather in this region of the heavens were seen by the ancient clairvoyants to form in the image of a man shouldering an urn of water, which he pours out in a steady, timely measure.

With the eurythmy gesture for Aquarius we honor the outer work of the Waterbearer. Our arms extend out and move up and down in a steady measured rhythm/cadence with our palms open toward the earth as though pouring forth the waters of cosmic grace.

Correspondingly, the eurythmy sound "M" expresses the inner quality of Aquarius – a *"touching into our surroundings with sympathy, giving and receiving harmoniously"*. Our palms face outwards toward our community, opening ourselves to send and receive the etheric streaming of Aquarius.

As we dance the cosmic dance of Aquarius to music in B♭ major or G minor, we can imagine the harmonizing effect of a total relaxation from all the rigidity of life, all the false structure. As we connect with love and a sense of true purpose, we imagine ourselves surrounded by a rose pink quality of color, through which the mood arises within that is expressed in the words: *"I feel the source of all life."*

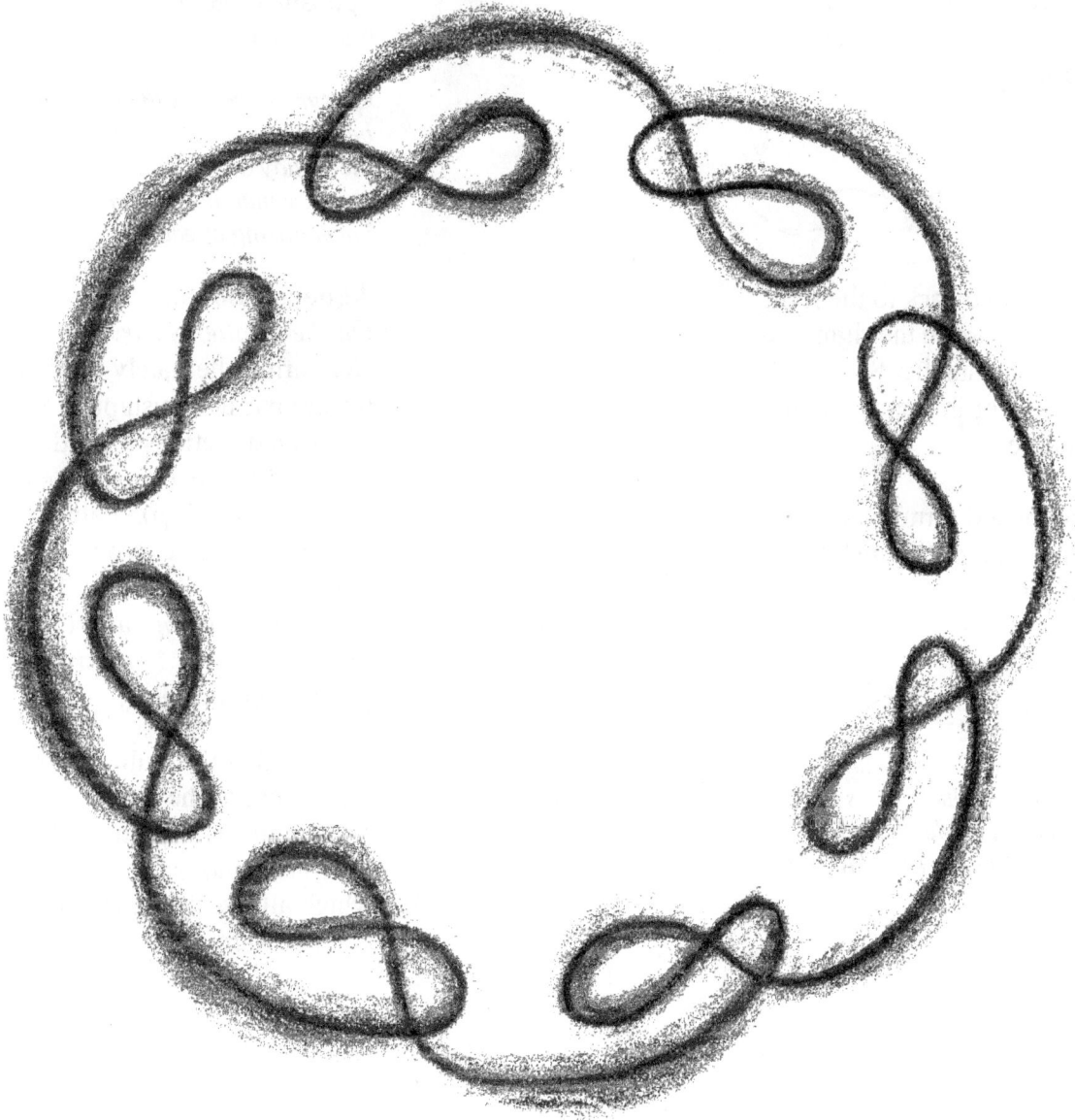

Aquarius Choreography

Aquarius Cosmic Dance Form
"Feeling the source of all life"

Aquarius *Eurythmy* Form:

Curve back to the left and forward to the left in an S curve.

Now curve back to the right and forward to the right making a smaller S curve that is a mirror image of the first S curve.

Completed form traces a lemniscatory (figure "8") pattern.

This steady forward and back movement which forms the pattern of the lemniscate emphasizes the use of the calves in the lower leg.

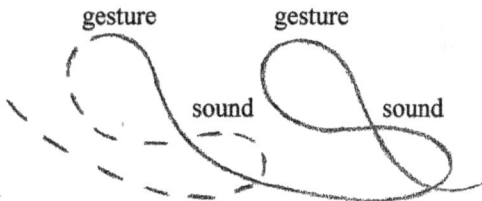

gesture gesture

sound sound

Continue moving back to the left and then forward to the left to form the larger S curve beginning the next figure "8" lemniscatory form.

Aquarius *Gesture*:
On large S curve to the left, arms extend out in front of body, R. arm raised, L. arm lowered (*palms open, facing earth*); move arms up and down in opposite directions in a slow and *even* rhythm.

Gesture expresses the breathing between heaven and earth and the steady outpouring of divine grace, which has an overall harmonizing effect.

Aquarius *Sound*: "M"
On the smaller S curve to the right arms alternately bend at the elbows and push/pull in opposite directions toward center of circle. (*Palms open, fingers pointed up*). Palm of extending arm faces out, (*away from body*) palm of pulling (*retracting*) arm faces in toward body. *A gesture of giving and receiving.*

The steady push/pull movement of the arms emphasizes the *opening of the wrists and forearms* which allows the hands to bend upward.

This opens etheric channels to send and receive etheric life forces via open palms and forearms.

Continue alternating arm movements: ***The Aquarius gesture*** *while moving to the left and the* **sound "M"** *while moving to the right.*

Aquarius – *"the Waterman" or "Waterbearer"*   (February 14 – March 15)
"Elixir of life and healing..."

Some say the "Waterbearer" relates to the image referred to by St. John as the *"sign of the Son of man in heaven"*, the Risen Christ, pouring out his *grace* to humankind in a never ending fount.[51] This is understood as the *"second coming"*, leading us into the Aquarian Age beginning in 2375 AD, the time when the vernal point enters the sign of Aquarius. The "second coming" signifies that the etheric body of the earth is receiving the *living waters* of the etheric body of Christ.[52]

The royal star ***Fomalhaut*** in the *Southern Fish* (9°♒) marks the mouth of the celestial fish which drinks/receives the waters which pour from the Waterman's urn. With Regulus (the heart of the Lion) in the North, Aldebaran (the Bull's Eye) in the East, and Antares (the heart of the Scorpion) in the West, <u>Fomalhaut</u> in *"The Great Fish"* completes the axis of the Four Royal Stars, the Guardians of Heaven, which are associated with the royal way, the path of initiation.

To complete this promise of living waters, it is inspiring to *drink* from the fountain of *wisdom* which flows as mother's milk from the stories foretold in the ancient legends and myths concerning Aquarius and Fomalhaut.

The Babylonians associated the region of the heavens which we call Aquarius with the Watergoddess, *Gula,* who poured water from two vessels onto the Earth from which arose the Tigris and the Euphrates rivers, the water beds which nourished their civilization.

Likewise, the Egyptians imagined Aquarius as the God of the Nile, who poured (again from *two vessels)* creating the Blue and the White Nile, the two great sources of the Nile.[53]

For the ancient Greeks the *"two vessels"* become one, with Aquarius representing *Deucalion*, the Greek Noah, associated with the "flood". The Greeks considered Deucalion to be the founder of the human race, who continues to pour out the waters which bless humankind.

Thus, the foretelling of the *"coming of the etheric Christ"* lived in the hearts and imaginations of the early peoples. With Fomalhaut the prefiguring of Sophia is also revealed.

---

[51] Robert Powell, *The Sign of the Son of Man in the Heavens.*
[52] The words of St John, "He is coming on the clouds", signify the pouring out of the waters of life (clouds symbolizing and bearing the life-giving water – outpictured in the form of rain – for the earth).
[53] The Blue source symbolizes the Solomon line of descent, the kingly stream, leading to the birth of the Solomon Jesus. The White source symbolizes the pure/heart stream of the Nathan Jesus. As a symbol, the Nile, wherein the two become one, represents the vessel for the Christ.

Early legends regarded the star Fomalhaut as representing "*The Great Fish*" associated with a Goddess who plunged into a holy lake (Earth). She was changed into this great fish which drinks from the grace-filled waters of the Waterman's urn.

This story becomes more vivid when we consider the Egyptian legend which foretold of *Isis* being saved by a "*great fish*". (In Christian tradition, Christ is the fish).

These ancient stories serve as vessels for the imagination of the pouring out of abundance from the great cosmic source, which we find archetypally in the story of the *Wedding at Cana*. Jesus, the bearer of the Christ, said to his Mother Mary, "*Woman what flows between us*" and then the jugs of water were transformed into *fine wine* for the wedding feast, a foretelling of the *sacred marriage* of Christ and Sophia described in <u>*The Revelation to John*</u>.

The Sun (10½°♒) was aligned with the mega star Deneb at the *feeding of the five thousand*. Deneb, with a luminosity 270,000 times that of our Sun, is the most powerful 1st magnitude star in our local part of the galaxy, the Orion Arm. It is also the star leading the way for our Sun and all the stars in the vicinity of our Sun, as our Sun and all the neighboring stars travel along their paths of orbit around the Galactic Center, the Central Sun. When we look up to Deneb marking the head of the Northern Cross (identified by the Greeks as the tail of the Swan), we can imagine a trajectory passing from our solar system through Deneb and sweeping along a great arc around the Galactic Center. The *feeding of the five thousand* is the fourth miracle described in the <u>*Gospel of St John*</u> and was immediately followed that same evening by the fifth miracle, *the walking on the water*, when the Sun was at 11° Aquarius. As well as being aligned with Deneb at both these miracles, the Sun was also close to the royal star Fomalhaut (9°♒) in the mouth of the Southern Fish. When Jesus walked on the water, he said to his disciples, "*Be not afraid, it is I,*" manifesting his royal nature as Lord of the Elements.

Aquarius – *"As above, so below."*   (February 14 – March 15)
     "On earth as it is in heaven."

The Birth of Purified Reflection

The sign for Aquarius, which mirrors the etheric flow through the stars of the constellation is represented by two undulating lines, one above the other suggesting the early teaching of **Hermes**, "*as above, so below*", and the words given in the Lords Prayer, "*On earth as it is in heaven*," foretelling the birth of purified reflection.

Both Rudolf Steiner and Valentin Tomberg were born when the Sun was in the *feeling* heart of Aquarius (14½°≈). Both of these great initiates and teachers bore the gift of discretion and spiritual discernment which come with the perfected powers of reflection extending beyond the disfiguring possibilities of atavistic imagination.

If we read the starry script which supports the etheric body of the Waterman, and contemplate the myths and legends surrounding this body of the heavens, we can glimpse a reflection of the central purpose and intentions of Aquarius which are reflected in the life work of these two great individualities.

The central region of Aquarius (2nd decan) is home to **Cygnus** *the Swan,* which forms a large and beautiful cross in the night sky (*the Northern Cross*). Both the Swan and the Cross are symbols of beauty, purity, dignity and grace. Thus, it is not surprising that this celestial Swan is known as the *Bird of Venus.* Under the aegis of Venus, there are concerns for beauty, art, music, nature, etc.[54]

In Greek legend the constellation of the Swan was associated with "*Leda*" the *Mother* of the Twins, the twin *brothers* of Gemini (Castor and Pollux), which reminds us of the blossoming of *Sophia* that accompanies the age of Aquarius, with concerns for *brotherhood* and community.

This celestial Swan with the structure of an *inner cross* is considered in esoteric teachings to be connected with the Grail mystery. This theme is beautifully portrayed in Wagner's opera, *Lohengrin* – where Lohengrin is drawn along and inspired by a *great swan* which guides his destiny.

If we contemplate the place of the Sun (11°≈) when the *walking on the water* took place, we find the bright star **Deneb** (10½°≈), which marks the tail of the Swan and correspondingly the head of the Cross, thereby creating an image of circling and returning.

With Deneb we can discover some rather awesome scientific findings. Firstly, Deneb whose *apparent* magnitude ranks it as 19th among the brightest visible stars in our night sky – is discovered to be, due to its enormous distance in light years from our solar system, actually the brightest 1st magnitude star (in an absolute sense) – having a luminosity at least 270,000 times greater than our Sun.

---

[54] Aeschylus sang, "the Swan expiring dies in melody, and true it is that the Swan upon dying emits a unique and melodious sound."

In the revelations to St. John on the island of Patmos, the white horse, the first of the four apocalyptic horses, represents our beginning in pure spirit. Thus, Deneb represents the future. It can be thought of as the omega star ("*I am the alpha and the omega*" – *The Revelation to John* 1:11).

The star Deneb in the constellation of the Swan (related to the central decan/region of Aquarius) is connected to the development of our *pineal gland*. This can be experienced directly, when one reaches toward this star with the sense of *spiritual touch*, which the etheric waters of Aquarius enliven. It is through a developed pineal gland that the gifts of spiritual perception are received (without distortion) by the imaginative faculties of man.

When we come to the final decan of Aquarius, we find another spiritual gift in the story of the myth of **Pegasus**, the winged, celestial horse, whose *head* marks the culminating region of Aquarius. Pegasus was named from *Pegai*, the springs of the ocean, the place of his birth. Pegasus was called *"horse of the fountain"* because he first appeared near the springs of the ocean. According to Willi Sucher, the winged white horse Pegasus – in the heavens appearing to spring from the head of Andromeda – signifies the *birth* of pure *imagination*.

In the revelations to St. John on the island of Patmos, the white horse, the first of the four apocalyptic horses, represents our beginning in pure spirit. The story of Pegasus is a foretelling of the work of the Cosmic Christ, providing the living waters born of imagination and freeing us from the paralyzing threat of the "turning stone into bread" – recalling that archetypally Christ is "the living bread which comes down from heaven" (*John* 6:51).

When we look up to the stars, we can think of the words of Isaiah: *"Lift up your eyes on high and see: who created these?"* *"He who brings out their host by number, calling them all by name"* (*Isaiah* 40:26). As a sign for this great work, the star **Situla** named by the Greek letter **Kappa,** marks the mid-point of Aquarius (14½° ≈≈), recalling the Sun's location for the birth of both ValentinTomberg and Rudolf Steiner (14½° ≈≈). Here we have an image of the pouring out of water to quench thirst, since *Situla*, meaning water jar, derives from the root word *situs* which means thirst, and as this star marks the mouth of the Waterbearer's urn, it bears the promise of an *outpouring*. Thinking of the spiritual teachers Rudolf Steiner and Valentin Tomberg, we have an image of the outpouring of wisdom for the Aquarian Age.

This image reveals the Love of the Cosmic Christ as the true healer, pouring forth the elixir of life, *"Whosoever drinks of the water that I shall give him will never thirst…it will become in him a spring of water welling up to eternal life"* (*John* 4:14).

Developing the capacity to connect with this living substance recalls the images of the two celestial messengers, **Pegasus** and the **Swan**, *returning swiftly with answers of purity and joy*, inspiring deeds of nobility, spawning inventions of sustaining value which work in harmony with nature, and a respectful, appropriate care of community and the brotherhood of man.

The Waterman's Urn

Consider the prophecy of the etheric Christ *"coming on the clouds"* – clouds might be considered like the Waterman's urn, in that they are containers of both air and water and live between the two elements by virtue of a state of *dynamic tension*. This is the challenge of the free flowing waters of Aquarius.

How to maintain a balance, a steadiness, a harmonization between the inpouring (inbreath) and the outpouring (outbreath), the taking in of sense experience and the pouring out of information. Water/Air – Verbalization/Silence. How to contain, how to *create* the container, how to discern boundaries in the boundaryless region called Aquarius.

The air waves are crowded with electronic competition for the free space of spiritual reality. In short, there is so much out there. How do we discern what to take in and what not to take in? And even more interesting, Aquarius is the region that challenges us to *discern* the qualities of what we take in.

The answer is found in the astrological sign which traces the etheric flowing in this region – two wavy lines, one floating above the other, a mirroring image, "As above, so below." The wavy lines suggest the flow of air and water into eternity. However, it is the relationship of the one to the other that is most apparent. Here again we have a calling for inner *silence*, a *stilling* of the waters in order to perceive rightly.

The Sun was in this region when Jesus walked on water saying to the disciples, *"Be not afraid, it is I"*. To still fear is the archetypal example for stilling the waters, creating a *container* of inner calm in order to receive inspiration or, as in this archetypal example, achieving *elevation*.

The planet **Saturn** is said to be at *home* in Aquarius because these are spiritual waters. Uranus also shares an important relationship to Aquarius. Uranus is the planet of invention, having to do with bringing the spiritual down into existence in earthly life, inspiring humanity to *create* a *container for spiritual substance*.

Aquarius Meditation Work: *"Overcoming self limitation."*

Sun in Aquarius: February 14 – March 15

"Discretion becomes silence > becomes meditative force > becomes power"

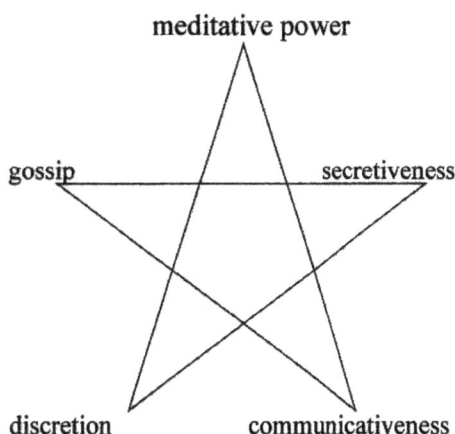

meditative power

gossip   secretiveness

discretion   communicativeness

Challenge: To temper the sense of boundless freedom with an alignment with truth and higher purpose guided and shaped by the power of LOVE.

Discretion requires the ability to separate and distinguish – which leads to spiritual discernment.

The lower two points provide the foundation required to achieve the higher aspect of Aquarius. The lower left-hand corner is the virtue. The lower right-hand corner is what is needed along with the virtue in order to arrive at the uppermost point. The mid-points are what the lower points become if taken to extremes.

Virtue: Discretion – *"Blessed are the discreet, for they shall have strength of mind."*
Sense: Warmth

Exercise: The goal of Aquarius: harmonious adaptations to the environment.

To give structure to the conservational imprint.

To develop *adaptability* – traditional customs, procedures, ideas, etc. are subject to revision, suspension or development.

Purified reflection indicates the function of one's Guardian Angel above and the work of the etheric body of Christ for the earth.

Affirmation: *"May the limited yield to the unlimited."*

World view: Pneumatism; pneuma, spiritual "air waves"; acting by means of wind or air; containing instrument for measuring air breathed at each moment. Having to do with discernment – cultivated through inner silence – refining the instrument of reception, spiritually and also with the "other", to discern the qualities of vibration.

Consider the competition posed by electronic devices to dominate etheric space (free air), and how one's inner space or container can become contaminated by toxic waste, in violation of the sanctity of inner silence.

Aquarius Individuals

Sun in **Aquarius**: *"May the limited yield to the unlimited."*

The Waterman is the macrocosmic image of the etheric body, which is the *waterbearer* in the human being, and thus has a special relationship to the etheric Christ.

Rudolf Steiner and Valentin Tomberg were born when the Sun was in the middle of the *Waterbearer*. Their lives are examples of a pouring out of creativity which is *sourced* from the highly developed meditative power and spiritual discernment which is required to reveal true spiritual truths without distortion and in service to the etheric Christ.

Further **Aquarius** individuals

first decan – Mercury – Piscis Australis (the Southern Fish)
King Henry VII of England (0½°), inventor and engineer Thomas Edison (0½°), Charles Darwin (1½°), President Abraham Lincoln (1½°), Roman Emperor Hadrian (4½°), English social philosopher Jeremy Bentham (5°), botanist and zoologist Ernst Haeckel (5½°), Theosophist Charles Leadbeater (5½°), Hindu mystic Ramakrishna (6°), French poet Rabelais (7°), Swedish explorer Sven Hedin (7½°), English playwright Christopher Marlowe (8°), Italian discoverer of electricity, Alessandro Volta (9°), composer Archangelo Corelli (9°), English humanist St. Thomas More (10°).

second decan – Venus – Cygnus (the Swan)
English theologian Cardinal Newman (10½°), German physicist Heinrich Hertz (11°), composer Frederic Chopin (11½°), German philosophers Karl Jaspers (11½°) and Schopenhauer (12°), President George Washington (12°), artist Renoir (14°), Wilhelm Grimm (Grimm's Fairy Tales) (14½°), author John Steinbeck (15°), transpersonal psychologist Robert Assagioli (15°), Italian tenor singer Enrico Caruso (15½°), French writer Victor Hugo (15½°), poet Longfellow (16°), Galileo (17½°), opera composer Rossini (19°), Pope Leo XIII (19°), inventor of the telephone, Alexander Graham Bell (19½°), Pope Pius XII (19½°), religious reformer Melanchthon (20°), mathematician Georg Cantor (20°).

third decan – Moon – Pegasus (the Winged Horse)
Astronomer Copernicus (23°), poet Elizabeth Barrett Browning (23½°), composers Maurice Ravel (24°), Vivaldi (24°), and Händel (25°), Emperor Charles V of Spain (26½°), Florentine humanist Pico della Mirandola (27½°), astronomer Urbain Leverrier (28°), poet Joseph von Eichendorff (29°), German philosopher and poet Friedrich von Schlegel (29°).

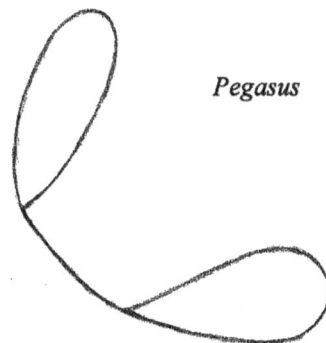

Pisces - Destiny

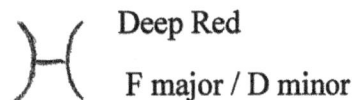

Deep Red

F major / D minor

The structure of the "inner cross" requires being fully born of the cosmos, which requires the completion of the descent of our *essential* essence into our physical being. With Pisces, we have finally reached our feet. Now the Tree of Life can fully breathe the *inner substance* of the "bread of life" – the substance which forms the inner organs, wherein the forces of youthfulness (life) and maturity (death) are brought into a state of balance.

Thus, the constellation of Pisces can be seen as a cosmic stream of nourishment, bestowing an *inner substance*, such that the organs of the physical body become capable of taking up spiritual life.[55]

Whereas the *head* of Pegasus graces the waters in the final region (decan) of Aquarius, the *body* of **Pegasus**, the celestial *source* of *imagination* and *inspiration* resides above the constellation of Pisces, especially above the beginning region (decan) of **the Fishes**. We see the body of Pegasus extending above the lower fish with his feet pointing upward toward heaven. This reminds us of the Pisces gesture in eurythmy and also of the Tarot Arcanum XII "The Hanged Man", which corresponds to the constellation of the Fishes.

Through the Pisces gesture one learns that the point of stability for the Piscean nature is the *upward* (heavenly) connection. It is the right hand (active) which consciously reaches for the heavenly connection that stabilizes the standing on one foot, symbolizing *one path* (destiny) firmly planted on the earth.

One can experience that the *tension* between the *upward reach* and the *earthly stance* creates a tenuous state of equilibrium, which requires a *constancy* of conscious, active choosing, as expressed in the Piscean sound "N". With this gesture we can imagine the cautious and delicate touch of a fish as it surfaces to obtain nourishment from above, sending out an eddying pattern in the water.

As we dance the eurythmy form for Pisces, our feet trace the pattern of the two fish – the one which swims heavenward, the other toward the future (Aquarius) – we create the form of a heart representing love, which is the *cord* of *heavenly accord* connecting the two fish.[56] We imagine ourselves surrounded by the deep red color associated with the heart shape (*recalling the wine of the blood of Christ*) as we dance to music written in the key of F major or D minor. The depth of the color red awakens the understanding that "*strength of will is rooted deep within.*"

---

[55] The twelve streams of cosmic nourishment comprising the "Tree of Life" are described in *Christian Hermetic Astrology*, pages 198–204.
[56] At the miracle of the feeding of the 5000, Venus was in Pisces (the two fish) and the Moon was in Virgo (the bread) and the Sun was in Aquarius in conjunction with Deneb in the constellation of the Swan.

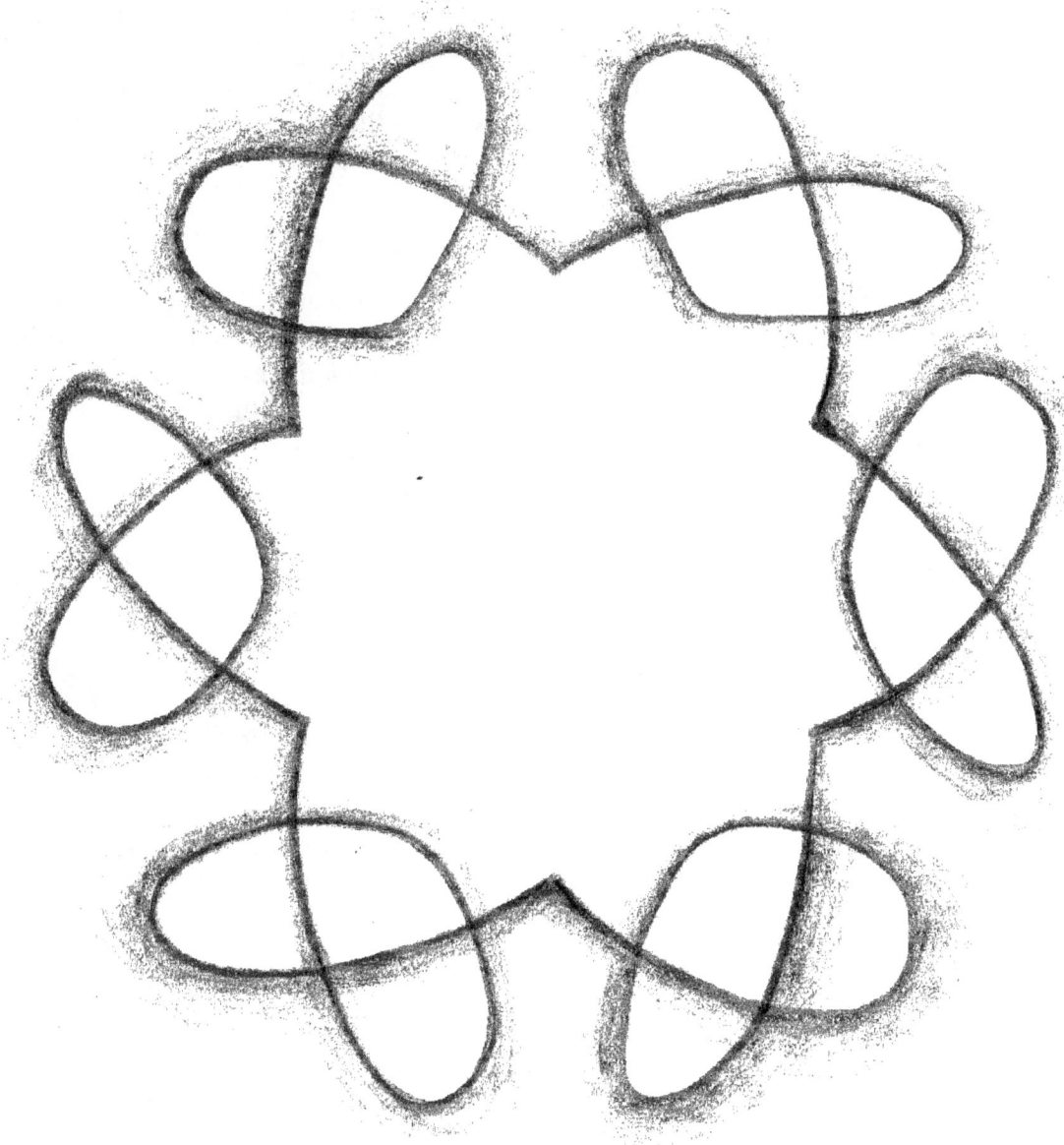

Pisces Choreography

Pisces Cosmic Dance Form

"Touching the phenomena around and withdrawing in order to understand"

Pisces *Eurythmy* Form:
The form for Pisces traces the shape of a heart.

Begin by moving back to the left, circling around and moving forward to the right, *forming the first fish.*

Continue moving to the right and back, then circle around and move forward to the left, *forming the second fish.*

On completion of the second fish, make Pisces gesture.

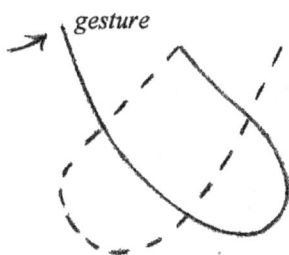

At the mid-point of the connecting cord, *the point of balance,* pause and stand with right foot raised slightly or lightly touching ground with toe *for balance.*

Pisces *Sound*: "N"
In the forming of the two fish, the sound "N" comes to completion at the farthest point (head) of each fish.

As you loop to the left slowly forming the left hand fish, bring the arms upward and then lightly touch downward, drawing back instantly, as though changing your mind in order to go in the opposite direction *while moving forward to the right.*

Repeat the "N" gesture while forming the second fish (*right hand fish*), completing the gesture at the head of the fish.

Touching the phenomena around and withdrawing in order to understand.

Pisces *gesture*: *At the central point of the cord which connects onto the next form,* stand on left foot, right foot raised slightly, toes pointed down...

with right arm extended straight up, *palm open, facing forward, fingers pointing toward heaven;*

left arm bends at elbow and is held with elbow lifted, *palm open, facing back, fingers pointing toward left foot.*

102

Pisces *"The Fishes"* (March 15 – April 15)
"The mystery of destiny."

The region of Pisces is connected in mythology to the descent of Hercules into the underworld to rescue Theseus. Thus, Pisces is connected to our awakening to Mother Earth and the forces of the underworld.

It is said that our feet "know" our future, so it is important to be conscious of where our feet take us. We see this in the formation of the stars in the region of the heavens known as Pisces which the ancient star gazers who possessed the faculty of clairvoyance imagined as two fish connected together by a cord with the *lower fish* swimming toward Aquarius (the *future*) and the *upper fish* swimming upward (*heavenward*).

In the age of Pisces in which we are now living (AD 215 to 2375), we are approaching the future age of Aquarius which will begin in the year 2375. The feet correspond to Pisces and our feet bear us toward the fulfillment of our destiny and our relationship to the future.

At present the vernal point rests at 5° Pisces. In accordance with the precession of the equinoxes, the vernal point moves backward approximately 1° every 72 years, and will enter into the region of the constellation of Aquarius in 2375. With the upper fish swimming toward heaven we have the mystery of *destiny* that is *written* in heaven and with the lower fish swimming toward Aquarius (the *future*) we have an image of destiny leading us into the future. The two fish are linked by a cord. Symbolically our destiny and heaven are inescapably linked. It is the heavenly power of love that flows through to the fulfillment of love.

It is interesting to recall that with the juxtaposition of the constellation of Aries (head) with the sign of Pisces (feet), we have the *head* touching the *feet*, the *alpha* and *omega* of continual existence. The circular image of the human form circled around the signs of the zodiac, with the feet in Pisces and the head in Aries, reminds us of the ancient symbol of the ouroborus, the dragon biting its tail.

We can recall that Jesus Christ, who brought the teaching of love to the Earth in the age of Aries and was referred to as the "*Lamb of God*", became connected with the image of the *Fish* when the vernal point entered Pisces in AD 215. The Sun was in Pisces at Jesus' triumphant entry into Jerusalem (29°♓) and when Peter received the keys to the kingdom (28½°♓). Interestingly, the planet Venus is exalted at 27° Pisces.

As with the myths associated with the constellations, the earlier myths of antiquity were also sometimes a foretelling of the future. So it is with the story of love in connection with the constellation of Pisces. According to an ancient myth, it was this watery region that birthed the fair ***Venus***, the planet that is said to be the "star of Aphrodite", the goddess who inspires the form of love that we associate with Eros. Jesus Christ brought the teaching of the metamorphosis of sensual love (*Eros*) into divine love (*Agape*)...his two commandments being, "*Love the Lord thy God with all thy heart and soul*" and "*love one another.*"

Venus was pursued by the Sea God Neptune who threatened to take her back to the sea which could be symbolically interpreted as *dissolution* into *illusion.* Herein lies one of the challenges of Pisces, that bears the gift of *psychic* perception, which must become consciously balanced with an active engagement with reality.

As well as Venus being exalted in Pisces, the constellation of the Fishes is ruled by the planet Jupiter. The planet of Zeus rules both Pisces and Sagittarius. In the case of Sagittarius the might intelligence of Jupiter/Zeus manifests in the Archer who tames the horse, representing the subconscious. The horse motif recurs with the winged horse Pegasus arching above Pisces – the winged horse representing intelligence (thus aligned with Jupiter).

The body of the heavenly horse **Pegasus** (imaged in the heavens by the *square* of Pegasus) is constellated above the lower fish (primarily the first decan of Pisces). Pegasus enhances the tendency toward mystical union which is stirred and enlivened by Pisces. Pegasus is called the "horse of the foundation", "the messenger of joy and glad song" under whose hoofs the Pierian Springs started on Mt. Helicon. Here we are reminded of appearances of Mary accompanied by the springing forth of healing waters.

Andromeda, *"the Chained Woman"* can also be seen in this region of Pisces with the winged horse Pegasus springing from her forehead. Perseus (representing the human *spirit*) saved fair *Andromeda* (representing the divine feminine or the *soul* of humanity) from being *swallowed* by the great celestial *Whale*, **Cetus** (representing the blind, instinctive forces of the subconscious). Perseus' deed came as a divine promise in support of the intention symbolized by the Upper Fish of Pisces which perpetuates our connection to heaven. (The upper region of Andromeda is located above the third decan of Pisces, where the Upper Fish is located.) It is also in this decan where Venus finds her place of exaltation at 27° ♓.

And finally, as a witness to love, the very *heart* of Pisces served as a cradle for the Sun at the *birth* of the *Solomon* Jesus (15½° ♓) – and at the *conception* of the *Nathan* Jesus (16° ♓). Thus, it is not surprising that in this central region of Pisces (middle decan), we find **Cepheus**, the *Crowned King,* the archetype of the wise king whose task it is to bring the heavenly law to Earth. In the right-hand side of the crown of Cepheus is the beautiful red supergiant known as the Garnet Star, which was aligned with the Sun at 15½° Pisces at the birth of the kingly (Solomon) Jesus. It is the reddest star visible to the naked eye in the northern sky, usually appearing a deep orange-red, but occasionally taking on a purple tint. With a luminosity over 46,000 times that of our Sun, this powerful mega star was the *birth star* of the Master Jesus in his incarnation as the Solomon Jesus, as distinct from the star Sirius, which is his *eternal star* (see footnote 25 on page 33).

Pisces Meditation Work: *"Magnanimity becomes love..."*

Sun in Pisces: March 15 – April 15

Virtue: Magnanimity – *"Blessed are the magnanimous, for they shall be filled with love."*

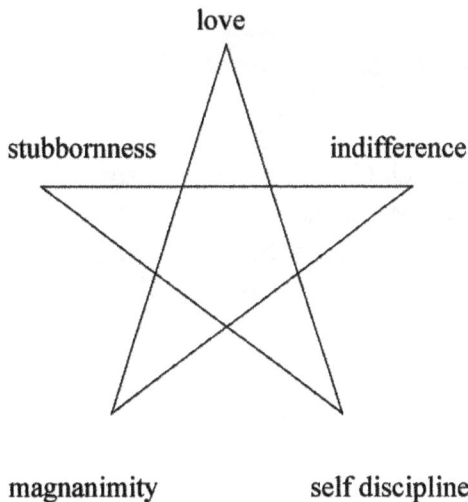

love

stubbornness   indifference

magnanimity   self discipline

Good Samaritan – lending a helping hand to save whoever is lost. Take care that your helping hand does not lead to getting "hooked" or to "hooking" another, which can lead to "burnout" (indifference).

"Cold feet" – difficulty in decision making: Here the challenge is to develop flexibility and openness to be able to change course or direction if conditions and life events call for it.

Important that the (often unconscious) "will to give" be prefaced by the question – where is this gift leading? Challenge to develop consciousness to steer your own ship to a particular destination without getting sidetracked by wanting to lend a helping hand.

The lower two points provide the foundation required to achieve the higher aspect of Pisces. The lower left-hand corner is the virtue. The lower right-hand corner is what is needed along with the virtue in order to arrive at the uppermost point. The mid-points are what the lower points become if taken to extremes.

Ideal: *"Not I, but Christ in me."* Challenge to be a "fisher of men" in the highest sense.
Pisces: Bread of Life – Inner substance – mystical connection.
Sense: Hearing – Universal language.

Tree of Life: The Holy Sacrament – "Give us this Day our Daily Bread". Take care that your "helping hand" does not rob another of a precious gift or opportunity to learn an important lesson.

World view: Psychism. The Piscean challenge is that of self delusion: it is important, in view of the inclination toward the mystical, to stay *grounded* in reality ("on your feet").

Historical Personalities
Sun in **Pisces**: *"In losing, may loss be found".*

first decan – Saturn –the Square of Pegasus (the Body of the Winged Horse)
Physicist Albert Einstein (0½°), Italian king Victor Emmanuel II (1°), French writer and philosopher Montaigne (1°), Emperor Joseph II (1½°), Pope Paul III (1½°), German physicist Georg Ohm (4½°), engineer and discoverer Rudolf Diesel (5°), Catholic theologian Hans Kung (5°), Russian philosopher Berdyaev (5°), Russian composer Rimsky-Korsakov (5°), "sleeping prophet" Edgar Cayce (5½°), German poet Friedrich Hebbel (5½°), composer Max Reger (5½°), Henry the Navigator (6°), painter and sculptor Michelangelo (6½°), Norwegian poet and playwright Henrik Ibsen (7½°), composer Modest Mussorgski (7½°), poet Holderlin (8½°), astrologer Dane Rudhyar (9°), poet and novelist Jean Paul (9°).

second decan – Jupiter – Cepheus (the Crowned King)
Composer Pierre Boulez (11°), poet Robert Hamerling (11°), composer Bela Bartok (11½°), astronomer and mathematician Laplace (12°), artist Van Dyck (12°), discoverer of X-rays, Röntgen (14°), Russian writer Maxim Gorky (15°), Master Jesus (also known as the Solomon Jesus) (15½°), Vincent Van Gogh (17°), poet Paul Verlaine (17½°), German chemist Robert Bunsen (18°), Spanish artist Goya (18½°), composer Ferrucio Busoni (18½°), German Chancellor Bismarck (19°), composer Rachmaninov (19°), Russian poet and writer Gogol (19°), Danish author Hans Christian Andersen (20°).

third decan – Mars – Andromeda
Composers Joseph Haydn (20½°) and Johann Sebastian Bach (21°), French philosopher Descartes (22°), Emperor Maximilian I (23°), German writer Bettina von Arnim (23½°), Romantic poet Wordsworth (26½°), Christian mystic St. Catherine of Sienna (26½°), French poet and writer Baudelaire (27°), artist Raphael (28°), Christian mystic St. Teresa of Avila (28°), homeopathist Hahnemann (28½°).

Afterword

ZODIAC MUSIC CD
Music for Meditation and for Cosmic Dance

This CD has been recorded by Russian concert pianist Ludmila Gricenko.[58] It has been made available as an aid to practice the cosmic dances of the zodiac when no musician (pianist or violinist) is available to accompany the cosmic eurythmy. It is always more preferable to move to live music, but in the event that this is not possible the Zodiac Music CD can be a help. As the title indicates, the CD can be used also for meditative purposes – attuning to the twelve signs of the zodiac, as each piece of music is in the key corresponding to a particular zodiacal sign. Working with the CD in Cosmic Dance is described below.

Correspondence of the musical keys with the zodiacal signs

On the CD Ludmila has recorded 24 pieces of music from the classical tradition: *two pieces for each sign of the zodiac*. Often the question is raised: For the cosmic dances, could one also move to modern music? The answer is that ideally someone would compose music especially for the cosmic dances. However, until there is specially composed music, it is necessary to take recourse to the extraordinary "treasure chest" of the classical tradition. The music of the great composers was composed out of an experience of the *harmony of the spheres*. This music is not arbitrary – it is a real expression of the heavenly music resounding in cosmic realms. The great classical composers (e.g. Bach, Mozart, Beethoven, Schubert, Chopin, Grieg) were able to capture – through their choice of musical key – something of the quality of the corresponding zodiacal sign. Prior to Rudolf Steiner's discovery (around 1920) of the correspondence between the musical keys and the zodiacal signs, the great composers were not *conscious* of this cosmic correspondence, but they grasped the qualities *intuitively*. At the time they were composing there was still a *living connection* with the spiritual realms from which music (as a reflection of the heavenly music of the harmony of the spheres) comes. In the twentieth century this connection was, by and large, lost (with a few notable exceptions). What was lost was the intuitive knowledge of the musical keys. As modern music, on the whole, is no longer composed in the framework of classical tonality – that of the twelve major and minor keys – it is not used in the Choreocosmos School for Cosmic and Sacred Dance, except in the case of modern compositions composed especially for eurythmy.

The twelve major and minor keys were used as a comprehensive "well tempered" musical system in the eighteenth century. Johann Sebastian Bach in his two volumes of preludes and fugues forming the *Well-Tempered Clavier* wrote two complete sets of

---

[58] Ludmila Gricenko, a concert pianist originally from St. Petersburg, has accompanied Robert Powell in workshops in Germany, Italy, Russia and Canada. Proceeds from the sale of the "Zodiac Music" CD are tax deductible and serve (through the efforts of a funding charitable foundation) to support the education of young musicians in Russia and to help Russian families in need. Phone from USA: 01149-8243-960700. Email: info@gricenko.de Website: www.gricenko.de

twenty-four pieces, one in each major and minor key, thereby helping to establish the remarkable scope of this tonal system underlying the classical tradition. However, although it was possible to transpose a piece from one key to another, the resulting transposition sounded different in the new key. The next step was the introduction of the equal tempered system of tuning the scale as twelve equal semitones, which gave the ability to transpose a musical piece to any key without changing its nature. This gain was made at a price – the loss of pure intervals, since the twelve precise semitones compromised the purity of harmony, with the equal tempered major thirds being slightly sharp and the fifths slightly flat. From that time onwards (1709, when the first piano was made) keyboard manufacturers favored the simplicity of equal temperament. Yet Bach's clavichord on which he composed *The Well-Tempered Clavier* (1722) was not equally tempered, but *well* tempered (as his work is titled). He composed the 48 pieces, two in each major and minor key, to show the character of each key in this temperament. This work has been referred to as the musical *Old Testament* (and Beethoven's 32 piano sonatas as the pianist's *New Testament*). Bach's intention in this work, laying the foundations of classical tonality, was to bring out the nuances of each key with its particular coloring. Although he did not <u>consciously</u> know it, his musical *Old Testament* mirrors here on earth the heavenly harmonies corresponding to the twelve signs of the zodiac. It is this – expressed in the correspondence of the twelve major and minor keys with the twelve signs of the zodiac – that underlies the classical tradition, and this correspondence was lost when this system of classical tonality was abandoned in the twentieth century.

The foregoing brief response to the question as to the use of the music of the classical tradition (rather than modern music) in the Choreocosmos School of Cosmic and Sacred Dance only touches the surface of a highly complex issue. Those who read German are encouraged to consult the works of Hermann Beckh and Friedrich Oberkogler for a more in-depth explanation of the correspondence between the twelve major and minor keys and the twelve signs of the zodiac.[59]

The 26 pieces on the Zodiac Music CD

The pieces are numbered #1 to #26:

1		**Grigori**		Expansion and Contraction
2	Aries	**Beethoven**	C Major	From the Waldstein Sonata, Op. 53
3	Aries	**Mozart**	C Major	Rondo
4	Taurus	**Chopin**	G Major	Prelude, Op. 28,3
5	Taurus	**Beethoven**	G Major	The Rage over the Lost Coin, Op. 129
6	Gemini	**Chopin**	D Major	From Mazurka, Op. 33,2
7	Gemini	**Schubert**	D Major	Sonata in D Major, 4th movement (theme)

---

[59] Hermann Beckh, <u>*Die Sprache der Tonart*</u> ("The Language of the Keys"). Beckh's book, published in 1937, was the first to explore the correspondence between the zodiacal signs and the twelve major and minor keys. Fifty years later, in 1987, Friedrich Oberkogler's comprehensive masterpiece *Tierkreis- und Planetenkräfte in der Musik* ("Zodiac and Planetary Forces in Music") was published in which he gives the musicological foundation of the zodiacal correspondence with the musical keys, supported by hundreds of examples drawn from the whole range of compositions from the classical tradition.

8	Cancer	**Mozart**	A Major	Variation IV from Sonata KV 331
9	Cancer	**Mozart**	A Major	Sonata in A Major KV 331, 1st movement (theme)
10	Leo	**Chopin**	E Major	From Étude Op. 10,3
11	Leo	**Schubert**	C# Minor	Impromptu Op. 90,4 (middle part)
12	Virgo	**Schubert**	B Major	Trio from Sonata in G Major Op. 78
13	Virgo	**Chopin**	B Major	Scherzo No. 1 Op. 20 (middle part)
14	Libra	**Chopin**	F# Major	Prélude Op. 28,13
15	Libra	**Schubert**	G♭ Major	Impromptu Op. 90,3 (theme)
16	Scorpio	**Chopin**	D♭ Major	From Nocturne Op. 27,2
17	Scorpio	**Chopin**	D♭ Major	Phantasy Impromptu (middle part)
18	Sagittarius	**Beethoven**	A♭ Major	From Sonata Op. 110 (theme)
19	Sagittarius	**Schubert**	A♭ Major	From Impromptu Op. 142,2
20	Capricorn	**Beethoven**	C Minor	Variation V from Op. 34
21	Capricorn	**Beethoven**	E♭ Major	Sonata Op. 27,1, 1st movement
22	Aquarius	**Schubert**	B♭ Major	Variation I from Impromptu Op. 142,3
23	Aquarius	**Schubert**	B♭ Major	Impromptu Op. 142,3 (theme)
24	Pisces	**Schubert**	D Minor	From Sonata in B♭ Major D 960
25	Pisces	**Gluck**	F Major	"Dance of the Blessed Spirits" from Orpheus and Eurydice
26		**Schuurman**		Expansion and Contraction

Direction of movement

In #2 below, reference is made to a map of our spiral galaxy (for example, the National Geographic map, October 1999). This map shows a representation of the estimated one hundred billion stars of the Milky Way galaxy dotted around four spiral arms (with side arms extending from the four main arms). All the stars rotate in a *clockwise direction* around the galactic center (**Central Sun**). This means that all the stars in the heavens, including all the stars comprising the twelve signs of the zodiac, are moving *clockwise*. For this reason the general direction of movement in all the cosmic dances of the zodiac is *clockwise*. A counter-clockwise movement may be part of the form (as in the example of Aquarius), but the *overall direction* of movement of the circle is clockwise. (In the cosmic dances of the planets, on the other hand, the overall direction of movement is *counter-clockwise*, in accordance with the general counter-clockwise movements of the Sun, Moon, and planets through the signs of the zodiac.) Thus, in the descriptions of the zodiacal cosmic dances the overall direction of movement is always clockwise.

Description of the CD pieces #1 to #26

With the exception of #1 and #26 (music for *Expansion and Contraction* as the opening and the closing exercise), there are **two pieces** of music for each sign of the zodiac (#2 to #25). **Moving to the first piece** is always *frontal*[59] – a *warming-up* and practicing of the zodiac gesture and the corresponding sound so as to enter into the mood of the zodiac sign. **Moving to the second piece of music** is *centered*[60] – moving the zodiac form together with the zodiac gesture and corresponding sound gesture.

---

[59] See description of *frontal* in # 2 below.

[60] *Centered* signifies that everyone – while moving – faces the center of the circle.

#1. The music by Grigori is composed to accompany the opening eurythmy exercise known as *Expansion and Contraction*.

Each participant moves together with the descending music toward the center of the circle bringing their hands – one cupped over the other – to their heart center and, at the same time, bending the upper body forward slightly, facing downward, in a gesture of contraction into oneself. The contraction represents interiorization, entering within to seek the core of one's being.

Then, together with the ascending music, one gradually straightens up while moving back to the periphery of the circle, at the same time bringing one's arms and hands up and opening outward in a gesture of expansion. The expansion represents exteriorization, reaching out to connect with the surrounding cosmos.

Expansion and Contraction is done as an opening exercise at the beginning, as a means of finding the path from the *spirit within* to the *spirit of the universe*. It is a way of attuning to the essence of the cosmic dances which then follow. It is also done as a closing exercise at the end (see #26).

#2. The participants stand in a circle, all facing in the same direction (*frontal*). It can be a help if there is some drawing or poster of a cosmic theme (a map of the solar system or the galaxy, for example) on the wall toward which everyone is facing. This can help the group to attune to the cosmos. A map of our spiral galaxy is a wonderful *mandala* in this respect.

When the Beethoven music in C major starts, the group begins to move together with the music in a clockwise direction, *each person remaining frontal whilst moving*. If a map of the spiral galaxy is on the wall toward which the group is facing, everyone can see it *the whole time* while moving around the circle, and all gestures are made *frontally* in that direction. The group endeavors to find together the right tempo, flowing along lightly (ethereally) with the music. It may take a while, but then usually the inner flow of the music can be felt as a stream carrying one around the circle in the right tempo.

Having found the right tempo, one adds to the movement the *Aries gesture* and the *gesture of the Aries sound* as described under the **Aries Cosmic Dance**. The gestures are made while the whole group continues to move clockwise in a lightly flowing circle. The Aries gesture is made when one is moving around the *back half* of the circle, and the gesture of the Aries sound when one is moving around the *front half* of the circle. A viewer watching this from the front sees, as the group of people (each facing the viewer frontally) moves flowingly around the circle, those in the front half of the circle *gesturing the sound "Vvvv"* **against the background** of those in the back half *holding the Aries gesture*. The viewer has the impression – through the gestures – of the Aries sound "Vvvv" issuing forth against the background of the sign of Aries. This creates the impression that the sign of Aries is *speaking forth* "Vvvv". As the circle is moving around there is a *continuous change* in the composition of the people comprising the *back half* (doing the Aries gesture) and the *front half* (doing the Aries sound "Vvvv").

The music in C major, the key of Aries, adds to the Aries mood created by the gestures of the participants as they move around the circle. The Aries mood is intensified still further by imagining the color red filling and permeating the room as one moves.

#3. Each participant turns to face the *center of the circle*. When the Mozart *Rondo* begins, each person moves the Aries (♈) form to the music – the first half of the ♈ form comprising movement to the left and back (opening half of the musical motif) and the second half of the ♈ form comprising movement forward and to the left (answering half of the musical motif).

(A) the Aries gesture is made while moving to the left and back.

(B) the gesture of the Aries sound "Vvvv" is made while moving forward and to the left.

(A) and (B) are repeated alternately, following each musical motif in Mozart's *Rondo*. The gestures are described under the **Aries Cosmic Dance**.

In practice, when a group is learning the cosmic dance of Aries, it is built up in three stages:

(i) learning to move the *Aries (♈) form*;

(ii) learning the *Aries gesture* while moving the first half of the form, and gently releasing the gesture while moving the second half of the form;

(iii) following the Aries gesture while moving the first half of the form, learning *the gesture of the Aries sound "Vvvv"* while moving the second half of the form.

#4. The participants stand in a circle *frontally* and start to move together clockwise around the circle with the music of Chopin's *Prelude*. The Taurus gesture is done by those moving around the back half of the circle, and the gesture for the Taurus sound "R" is done by those moving around the front half of the circle. As described in #2 for the cosmic dance of Aries, the goal is to move with the inner flow of the music.

#5. Each participant turns to face the *center of the circle*. When the Beethoven music begins, each person moves the Taurus (♉) form to the music – the first half of the ♉ form comprising movement to the left and back and around to the back of the circle (opening half of the musical motif) and the second half of the ♉ form comprising movement forward to the right and then to the left around the circle (answering half of the musical motif). See description #3 and **Taurus Cosmic Dance**.

#6. The participants stand in a circle *frontally* and start to move together clockwise around the circle with the music from Chopin's *Mazurka*. The Gemini gesture is done by those moving around the back half of the circle, and the gesture for the Gemini sound "H" is done by those moving around the front half of the circle. As described in #2 for the cosmic dance of Aries, the goal is to move with the inner flow of the music.

#7. Each participant turns to face the *center of the circle*. When the music from Schubert's *Sonata* (remaining standing for the introductory bars) begins, each person moves the Gemini (♊) form to the music – the first half of the first loop of the ♊ form comprising movement to the left and back (opening half of the musical motif) and the second half of the first loop of the ♊ form comprising movement forward to the right and then to the left (answering half of the musical motif). With the next musical motif, the second loop of the ♊ form is moved. See description #3 and **Gemini Cosmic Dance**.

#8. The participants stand in a circle *frontally* and start to move together clockwise around the circle with the music from Mozart's *Sonata*. The Cancer gesture is done by those moving around the back half of the circle, and the gesture for the Cancer sound "F" is done by those moving around the front half of the circle. As described in #2 for the cosmic dance of Aries, the goal is to move with the inner flow of the music.

#9. Each participant turns to face the *center of the circle*. When the music from Mozart's *Sonata* begins, each person moves the Cancer (♋) form to the music – the first half of the ♋ form comprising movement to the left and spiraling around clockwise (opening half of the musical motif) and the second half of the ♋ form comprising movement spiraling around counter-clockwise starting back to the left then to the right and then to the left (answering half of the musical motif). See description #3 and *Cancer Cosmic Dance*.

#10. The participants stand in a circle *frontally* and start to move together clockwise around the circle with the music from Chopin's *Étude*. The Leo gesture is done by those moving around the back half of the circle, and the gesture for the Leo sound "T" is done by those moving around the front half of the circle. As described in #2 for the cosmic dance of Aries, the goal is to move with the inner flow of the music.

#11. Each participant turns to face the *center of the circle*. When the music from Schubert's *Impromptu* begins, each person moves the Leo (♌) form to the music – the first part of the ♌ form comprising movement forward and then back to the left (opening part of the musical motif), the next part of the ♌ form comprising movement curving back and then forward to the left (next part of the musical motif), and the last part of the ♌ form comprising movement forward and then spiraling counter-clockwise around the Lion's heart (last part of the musical motif). See description #3 and *Leo Cosmic Dance*.

#12. The participants stand in a circle *frontally* and start to move together clockwise around the circle with the music from Schubert's *Sonata* (remaining standing for the introductory bars). The Virgo gesture is done by those moving around the back half of the circle, and the gesture for the Virgo sound "B" is done by those moving around the front half of the circle. As described in #2 for the cosmic dance of Aries, the goal is to move with the inner flow of the music.

#13. Each participant turns to face the *center of the circle*. When the music from Chopin's *Scherzo* begins, each person moves the Virgo (♍) form to the music – the first half of the first circle of the ♍ form comprising movement forward to the right and around to the left to the front of the circle (opening half of the musical motif) and the second half of the first circle of the ♍ form comprising movement back to the left and then to the right around the circle (answering half of the musical motif). With the next musical motif, the second circle of the ♍ form is moved. See description #3 and *Virgo Cosmic Dance*.

#14. The participants stand in a circle *frontally* and start to move together clockwise around the circle with the music of Chopin's *Prélude*. The Libra gesture is done by those moving around the back half of the circle, and the gesture for the Libra sound "Ts" is done by those moving around the front half of the circle. As described in #2 for the cosmic dance of Aries, the goal is to move with the inner flow of the music.

#15. Each participant turns to face the *center of the circle*. When the Schubert *Impromptu* begins, each person moves the Libra (♎) form to the music – the first part of the ♎ form comprising movement forward and then back to the left (opening half of the musical motif) and the last part of the ♎ form comprising movement forward and then back to the left (answering half of the musical motif). See description #3 and *Libra Cosmic Dance*.

#16. The participants stand in a circle *frontally* and start to move together clockwise around the circle with the music from Chopin's *Nocturne*. The Scorpio gesture is done by those moving around the back half of the circle, and the gesture for the Scorpio sound "S" is done by those moving around the front half of the circle. As described in #2 for the cosmic dance of Aries, the goal is to move with the inner flow of the music.

#17. Each participant turns to face the *center of the circle*. When the music from Chopin's *Phantasy Impromptu* (remaining standing for the introductory bars) begins, each person moves the Scorpio (♏) form to the music – the first part of the ♏ form comprising movement backward to the left and then forward to the right (opening half of the musical motif – ascending melody) and the last part of the ♏ form comprising movement backward to the left and then forward to the left (answering half of the musical motif – descending melody). See description #3 and *Scorpio Cosmic Dance*.

#18. The participants stand in a circle *frontally* and start to move together clockwise around the circle with the music from Beethoven's *Sonata* (remaining standing for the introductory bars). The Sagittarius gesture is done by those moving around the back half of the circle, and the gesture for the Sagittarius sound "G" is done by those moving around the front half of the circle. As described in #2 for the cosmic dance of Aries, the goal is to move with the inner flow of the music.

#19. Each participant turns to face the *center of the circle*. When the music from Schubert's *Impromptu* begins, each person moves the Sagittarius (♐) form to the music – the first part of the ♐ form comprising movement backward to the right (first part of the musical motif), the second part of the ♐ form comprising movement continuing to the left (second half of the musical motif) and the last part of the ♐ form comprising movement forward to the right (last part of the musical motif). See description #3 and *Sagittarius Cosmic Dance*.

#20. The participants stand in a circle *frontally* and start to move together clockwise around the circle with the music from Beethoven. The Capricorn gesture is done by those moving around the back half of the circle, and the gesture for the Capricorn sound "L" is done by those moving around the front half of the circle. As described in #2 for the cosmic dance of Aries, the goal is to move with the inner flow of the music.

#21. Each participant turns to face the *center of the circle*. When the music from Beethoven's *Sonata* begins, each person moves the Capricorn (♑) form to the music – the first part of the ♑ form comprising movement straight forward (opening three notes of the musical motif) and the last part of the ♑ form comprising movement backward to the left and then circling around to the tail of the Goat (remaining part of the musical motif). See description #3 and **Capricorn Cosmic Dance**.

#22. The participants stand in a circle *frontally* and start to move together clockwise around the circle with the music from Schubert's *Impromptu*. The Aquarius gesture is done by those moving around the back half of the circle, and the gesture for the Aquarius sound "M" is done by those moving around the front half of the circle. As described in #2 for the cosmic dance of Aries, the goal is to move with the inner flow of the music.

#23. Each participant turns to face the *center of the circle*. When the music of Schubert's *Impromptu* begins, each person moves the Aquarius (♒) form to the music – the first part of the ♒ form comprising movement in a wave form back to the left and then forward to the left (first half of the musical motif) and the second part of the ♒ form comprising movement in a wave form back to the right and then forward to the right (second half of the musical motif). See description #3 and **Aquarius Cosmic Dance**.

#24. The participants stand in a circle *frontally* and start to move together clockwise around the circle with the music from Schubert's *Sonata*. The Pisces gesture is done by those moving around the back half of the circle, and the gesture for the Pisces sound "N" is done by those moving around the front half of the circle. As described in #2 for the cosmic dance of Aries, the goal is to move with the inner flow of the music.

#25. Each participant turns to face the *center of the circle*. When the music of Gluck's "Dance of the Blessed Spirits" begins, each person moves the Pisces (♓) form to the music – the first part of the ♓ form comprising movement in an elongated form back to the left and then forward to the right (first half of the musical motif) and the second part of the ♓ form comprising movement in an elongated form back to the right and then forward to the left (second half of the musical motif). See description #3 and **Pisces Cosmic Dance**.

#26. The music by Schuurman is composed to accompany the closing eurythmy exercise known as *Expansion and Contraction*. One moves forward (contraction) with the first four notes (1st bar). When the first note of the 2nd bar is played, one begins to move back (expansion). Continue expansion and contraction as described in #1.

An additional possibility is to include the words of Rudolf Steiner's *Twelve Moods* in between the two pieces of music for each sign of the zodiac.

"Twelve Moods" by Rudolf Steiner

Aries

SUN   Arise, O shining light,
VENUS   Take hold of growth's being,
MERCURY Lay hold of forces weaving,
MARS   Ray out awakening life.
JUPITER In face of resistance, succeed –
SATURN In stream of time, recede.
MOON   O shining light, abide!

Taurus

SUN   Become bright, radiant being,
VENUS   Feel growth's power.
MERCURY Weave life's thread
MARS   In creative world existence,
JUPITER In thoughtful revelation,
SATURN In shining life-contemplation.
MOON   O radiant being, appear!

Gemini

SUN   Reveal thyself, Sun life,
VENUS   Set repose in movement,
MERCURY Embrace joyful striving
MARS   Towards life's mighty weaving,
JUPITER Towards blissful world-knowing,
SATURN Towards fruitful ripe-growing.
MOON   O Sun life, endure!

Cancer

SUN   Thou resting, glowing light,
VENUS   Create life warmth,
MERCURY Warm soul life
MARS   To gain strength in test of trial,
JUPITER To become spirit permeated,
SATURN In peaceful light created.
MOON   Thou glowing light, become strong!

Leo

SUN   Irradiate with senses' might
VENUS   Existing ground of worlds,
MERCURY Feeling being's essence
MARS   To firmly willed existence.
JUPITER In stream of life flowing,
SATURN In weaving pain of growing,
MOON   With senses' might, arise!

Virgo

SUN   Behold worlds, O soul!
VENUS   May the soul fathom worlds,
MERCURY May the spirit penetrate being,
MARS   Work with powers of life,
JUPITER Build upon experiences undergone,
SATURN Trust in blossoming worlds to come.
MOON   O soul, know thou beings!

Libra

SUN   Worlds sustain worlds,
VENUS   In being experience being,
MERCURY In existing embrace existence.
MARS   And being effects being
JUPITER To pour forth deeds unfolding,
SATURN In world enjoyment reposing.
MOON   O worlds, uphold worlds!

Scorpio

SUN   Existence consumes being,
VENUS   Yet in being existence endures.
MERCURY In activity growth disappears,
MARS   In growth activity persists.
JUPITER In chastising world-activation,
SATURN In punishing self-formation,
MOON   Being sustains beings.

Sagittarius

SUN   Growth attains power of existence,
VENUS   In existence growth's power dies.
MERCURY Attainment concludes joyful striving
MARS   In life's active force of will.
JUPITER World-activity matures in dying,
SATURN Forms vanish in re-forming.
MOON   May existence feel existence!

Capricorn

SUN   May the future rest upon the past.
VENUS   May the past feel the future
MERCURY To be strong in the present.
MARS   In face of life's inner resistance
JUPITER May world-being's vigilance grow in power,
SATURN May the might of life's activity flower,
MOON   May the past bear the future!

Aquarius

SUN   May the limited yield to the unlimited.
VENUS   What lacks boundaries should found
MERCURY Boundaries in its own depths,
MARS   And should arise in life's stream,
JUPITER As a flowing wave self-sustaining,
SATURN In coming to existence self-shaping.
MOON   Limit thyself, O unlimited!

Pisces

SUN   In losing may loss be found,
VENUS   In winning may gain be lost,
MERCURY In comprehending seek to grasp
MARS   And maintain in maintaining.
JUPITER Through coming to existence upraised,
SATURN Through existing to become interlaced,
MOON   May loss be gain in itself!

These twelve mantric verses derive from Rudolf Steiner's clairvoyant perception of the passage of the planets against the background of the constellations of the zodiac. Each verse contains seven lines, one line for each of the seven classical planets. For example, the line for the Sun in Aries is "Arise, O shining light". This line expresses the nature of the Sun in the zodiacal sign of Aries. The quality of the Sun in Aries is that of *sunrise*. These 84 lines for the seven planets in the twelve zodiacal signs form the basis for the series of 84 cosmic dances of the **planets in the signs of the zodiac**, which comprise the content of the advanced level of the Choreocosmos School of Cosmic and Sacred Dance.

Working with the "Twelve Moods"

In the context mentioned above – the introductory level of the Choreocosmos School – it is possible to work with the "Twelve Moods" *in between* the two pieces of music for each sign of the zodiac. In the case of Aries, for example, after the Aries Beethoven music (see #2) finishes, each participant turns to face the *center of the circle*. Then each person moves the Aries (♈) form to the Aries verse – the first half of the ♈ form to the words "Arise" and the second half of the ♈ form to the words "O shining light". After completion of the ♈ form for the Sun in Aries, the ♈ form is repeated six more times – once for each of the remaining lines (Venus, Mercury, Mars, Jupiter, Saturn, Moon) of the Aries verse. See description #3 and *Aries Cosmic Dance*.

After the completion of moving the ♈ form seven times to the recital of the seven lines of the Aries verse, each participant remains facing the *center of the circle*. Then the Mozart *Rondo* begins, and each person moves the Aries (♈) form to the music – the first half of the ♈ form comprising movement to the left and back (opening half of the musical motif) and the second half of the ♈ form comprising movement forward and to the left (answering half of the musical motif), as described in #3 above.

In this way the Aries verse is inserted in between the two pieces of music for Aries. Of course, just as a pianist has to be present to play the two pieces of music (unless the CD is used), so also someone has to recite the Aries verse at the right tempo for the movement around the ♈ form for each line of the verse. It is best if the person reciting knows the verse by heart.

Correspondingly, the relevant zodiac verse can be inserted *in between* the two pieces of music for the remaining eleven signs of the zodiac in the same way as with Aries.

If the entire sequence of twelve signs is worked with choreocosmically in this way: music—verse—music, it takes somewhere between one hour and 1 ½ hours to complete this entire "cosmic liturgy" of the zodiac. This is a wonderful and fulfilling experience!

Choreocosmos School of Cosmic and Sacred Dance

offers a training in the cosmic dances of the four elements, the seven planets, and the twelve signs of the zodiac, as well as in sacred dance, moving to prayers and sacred texts. For further information, write or contact:

Sophia Foundation of North America

Email: sophia@sophiafoundation.org

Website: www.sophiafoundation.org

Bibliography

Richard Hinckley Allen, *Star Names: Their Lore and Meaning* (Dover Publications: New York, 1963)

Anonymous, *Meditatations on the Tarot: A Journey into Christian Hermeticism* (Tarcher/PenguinPutnam: New York, 2002)

Hermann Beckh, *Die Sprache der Tonart in der Musik von Bach bis Bruckner* (Urachhaus Verlag: Stuttgart, 1977)

Peggy W. Brill, *The Core Program* (Bantam Books: New York, 2001)

Ethelbert W. Bullinger, *The Witness of the Stars* (Kregel Publications: Grand Rapids/MI, 1967)

Harry F. Darling, *Essentials of Medical Astrology* (American Federation of Astrologers: Tempe/AZ, 1981)

Jacques Dorsan, *Votre Signe Astrologique n'est pas celui que vous croyez* (Editions Garancière: Paris, 1985)

Beinsa Douno, *Dans le Royaume de la Nature Vivante* (Le Courrier du Livre: Paris, 1966)

Beinsa Douno, *Paneurythmy* (Vsemir: Sofia/Bulgaria, 1993)

Isadora Duncan, *The Art of Dance* (Theatre Art Books: Sheldon Cheney/NY, 1969)

W. M. Flinders Petrie, *The Religion of Ancient Egypt* (Archibald Constable & Co.: London, 1908)

Wilhelm Gundel, *Neue astrologische Texte des Hermes Trismegistos* (Gerstenberg Verlag: Hildesheim, 1978)

Johanna Keyserlingk, *The Birth of a New Agriculture: Koberwitz 1924* (Temple Lodge Press: London, 1999)

Jacques Lusseyran, *Against the Pollution of the I* (Parabola Books: New York, 1999)

Rael & Mary Elizabeth Marlow, *Being and Vibration* (Council Oak Books: Tulsa/OK, 1993)

Friedrich Oberkogler, *Tierkreis- und Planetenkräfte in der Musik: Vom Geistgehalt der Tonarten* (Novalis Verlag: Schaffhausen, 1987)

Paul Platt, *The Qualities of Time: Contributions towards a Modern Understanding of how the Cosmos Works in Man* (privately published: Sheffield/MA, 1986)

Robert Powell, *Christian Hermetic Astrology: The Star of the Magi and the Life of Christ* (Anthroposophic Press: Gt. Barrington/MA, 1998)

Robert Powell, *Chronicle of the Living Christ: The Life and Ministry of Jesus Christ: Foundations of Cosmic Christianity* (Anthroposophic Press: Gt. Barrington, 1996)

Robert Powell, *Hermetic Astrology, vol.I: Astrological Reincarnation* (Hermetika: Kinsau/Germany, 1987)

Robert Powell, *Hermetic Astrology, vol.II: Astrological Biography* (Hermetika: Kinsau/Germany, 1989)

Robert Powell, *The Christ Mystery: Reflections on the Second Coming* (Rudolf Steiner College Press: Fair Oaks/CA, 1999)

Robert Powell, *The Sign of the Son of Man in the Heavens: Sophia and the New Star Wisdom* (SunCross Press: Vancouver/BC, 1999)

Robert Powell, *The Zodiac: A Historical Survey* (Astro Communications Services: San Diego/CA, 1984)

Robert Powell & Peter Treadgold, *The Sidereal Zodiac* (American Federation of Astrologers: Tempe/Arizona, 1985)

Vanda Sawtell, *The Medicine of the Stars* (Essential Nutrients: London, 1969)

Joseph A. Seiss, *The Gospel in the Stars* (Kregel Publications: Grand Rapids/MI, 1972)

Rudolf Steiner, *Ancient Myths: Their Meaning and Connection with Evolution* (Rudolf Steiner Press: London, 1971)

Rudolf Steiner, *Eurythmy as Visible Music* (Rudolf Steiner Press: London, 1977)

Rudolf Steiner, *Eurythmy as Visible Speech* (Rudolf Steiner Press: London, 1984)

Willi Sucher, *Cosmic Christianity & the Changing Countenance of Cosmology* (Anthroposophic Press: Hudson/NY, 1993)

Jim Tester, *A History of Western Astrology* (Ballentine Books: New York, 1989)

David Tresemer, *Conscious Movement: Eurythmy for Beginners* (All Seasons Chalice: Boulder/CO, 1996)

(*Meditations on the Tarot* and the books by Robert Powell are available from the Sophia Foundation of North America)

Astronomical Data
used in <u>*Cosmic Dances of the Zodiac*</u>
in grateful acknowledgement of
Peter Treadgold (1943-2005)

Readers of <u>*Cosmic Dances of the Zodiac*</u> can be grateful to Peter Treadgold as the creator of *Astrofire*, the computer program he wrote for research into Astrosophy (*Astro-Sophia*). In relation to Sophia, Divine Wisdom, perhaps it is interesting to know that the origin of the name *Astrofire* is described by Daniel Andreev (1906-1959), the great Russian poet and seer, in one of his visions. He beheld Sophia descending from the "*heights of our universe*", from the realm of the galaxy with its great center:

> *I vaguely remember seeing a glowing mist of stunning majesty, as though the creative heart of our universe had revealed itself to me in visible form for the first time. It was* ***Astrofire****, the great center of our galaxy.*[1]

The information given in this book concerning the Sun's zodiacal location at the birth of significant historical personalities according to decan and degree within the twelve signs/constellations is from the *Astrofire* database. Also, the information given concerning individual stars – for example, Rigel, as one of the mega stars (see page 24) – is from the *Astrofire* star catalogue.

Astrofire is used by many researchers around the world and is available from the Sophia Foundation. It is a far-reaching creation opening up extraordinary possibilities for research – containing a database of birth and death dates of historical personalities as well as a star catalogue with over 4000 stars. "*To me* ***Astrofire*** *is a very profound spiritual vision which I have been in the process of creating over many years*" (Peter Treadgold, quoted from the tribute to Peter in the <u>*Christian Star Calendar 2006*</u>).

Peter worked on developing *Astrofire* for a great many years. The inspiration for creating this program came through his contact with Willi Sucher (1902-1985), who pioneered Astrosophy. Those users of *Astrofire* who are doing research in the field of Astrosophy (*Star Wisdom*) will know what a remarkable instrument Peter has created.

Here it is a matter of honoring Peter's great spirit and his unique gift to humanity, to which we owe also the yearly <u>*Christian Star Calendar*</u> that gives the positions of the Sun, Moon and planets day by day – geocentrically and heliocentrically – in relation to events in the life of Christ.

---

[1] Daniel Andreev, *The Rose of the World* (Lindisfarne Books: Gt. Barrington/ MA, 1997), p. 198.

Planetary Rulers of the Decans and Zodiacal Signs

Zodiacal Sign	Planetary Ruler	Planetary Exaltation	Decan Ruler	
Aries	Mars	Sun at 19°	1	Mars
			2	Sun
			3	Mercury
Taurus	Venus	Moon at 3°	1	Venus
			2	Moon
			3	Saturn
Gemini	Mercury		1	Jupiter
			2	Mars
			3	Sun
Cancer	Moon	Jupiter at 15°	1	Mercury
			2	Venus
			3	Moon
Leo	Sun		1	Saturn
			2	Jupiter
			3	Mars
Virgo	Mercury	Mercury at 15°	1	Sun
			2	Mercury
			3	Venus
Libra	Venus	Saturn at 21°	1	Moon
			2	Saturn
			3	Jupiter
Scorpio	Mars		1	Mars
			2	Sun
			3	Mercury
Sagittarius	Jupiter		1	Venus
			2	Moon
			3	Saturn
Capricorn	Saturn	Mars at 28°	1	Jupiter
			2	Mars
			3	Sun
Aquarius	Saturn		1	Mercury
			2	Venus
			3	Moon
Pisces	Jupiter	Venus at 27°	1	Saturn
			2	Jupiter
			3	Mars

Planetary rulers of the decans: the references to Mercury and Venus signify the designations for these planets given in modern astronomy and not in the ancient Egyptian tradition where the names are reversed. Lacquanna Paul & Robert Powell, *Cosmic Dances of the Planets* (Sophia Foundation Press, 2007) includes a detailed discussion of the planetary rulers of the signs.

See next page for **Correspondences to the Twelve Signs of the Zodiac.**

CORRESPONDENCES TO THE TWELVE SIGNS OF THE ZODIAC

	SIGN	COLOR	SOUND	BODY	KEY	CAPACITY	INNER GESTURE	IMPULSE	VIRTUE
Aries	♈	Red	V,W	head	CM / am	awaken "I AM" consciousness	uprightness *thinking*	action has become the event	Devotion *self-sacrifice*
Taurus	♉	Orange	R	larynx/ throat	GM / em	will, speech, firmness	self-assertion *attunement*	action — the deed	Inner Balance *progress*
Gemini	♊	Yellow	H,Y	shoulders/ arms	DM / bm	balance between thinking & willing	judgement *symmetry*	capacity for action	Endurance *faith*
Cancer	♋	Green	F	ribcage/ breast	AM / f#m	empathy, nurturing	enfolding *embracing*	initiative impulse to action	Selflessness *catharsis*
Leo	♌	Blue	T,D	heart/ back	EM / c#m	warmth of heart, giving direction	unfolding life *openness*	fiery enthusiasm	Compassion *freedom*
Virgo	♍	Indigo	B,P	stomach/ womb/ intestines	BM/C♭M g#m/a♭m	protection of creative force of life	digestion of knowledge, new life arising	reasonable soberness	Courtesy *tact of heart*
Libra	♎	Violet	C,Ch,Ts	abdomen/ pelvis/hips	F#M/G♭M d#m/e♭m	justice, equity fairness	equilibrium *balance*	weighing of pros & cons in one's thought	Contentment *equanimity*
Scorpio	♏	Blue Lilac	S,X,Z	lower body genitals	C#M/D♭M a#m/b♭m	dynamic metamorphosis	commanding force, *attraction*	resolve of thought, sending it into the world	Patience *insight*
Sagittarius	♐	Red Lilac	G,K,J,Q	thighs	A♭M Fm	evolving toward goal	creative soul *taking aim*	resolution moves toward expression	Self-discipline *know the truth*
Capricorn	♑	Peach Blossom	L	knees	E♭M Cm	striving from past to future	encountering resistance, *the will affirms itself*	thought struggles with conditions of outer world	Courage *power to redeem*
Aquarius	♒	Rose	M	calves	B♭M gm	overcoming self-limitation	balance of thinking, *feeling and will/seeks*	synthesis that equilibrium	Discretion *strength of mind*
Pisces	♓	Deep Red	N	feet	FM dm	rebirth, evolving essence of being	consciousness *creativity*	the event has become destiny	Magnanimity *love*

Astrofire Computer Program for Charts and Ephemerides

With grateful acknowledgment to Peter Treadgold, who wrote this computer program that includes a research module, star catalog of over 4000 stars, and database of birth and death charts of historical personalities, and which is capable of printing out geocentric and heliocentric/hermetic sidereal charts and ephemerides throughout history.

With this program one can:

- o compute birth charts in a large variety of systems (tropical, sidereal, geocentric, heliocentric, Tychonic/hermetic);* calculate conception charts using the hermetic rule, in turn applying it for correction of the birth time; produce charts for the period between conception and birth, and print them out in color
- o print out an "astrological biography" for the whole of life with the geocentric, heliocentric (and even lemniscatory) planetary system
- o work with the sidereal zodiac according to the definition of your choice (Babylonian sidereal, Indian sidereal, unequal-division astronomical, etc.)
- o work with planetary aspects with orbs of your choice

Included are eight house systems and a variety of chart formats, as well as an ephemeris program with a search facility. This program runs under Microsoft Windows.

If you are interested in *Astrofire*, please contact the Sophia Foundation of North America (see contact information at the beginning of this book).

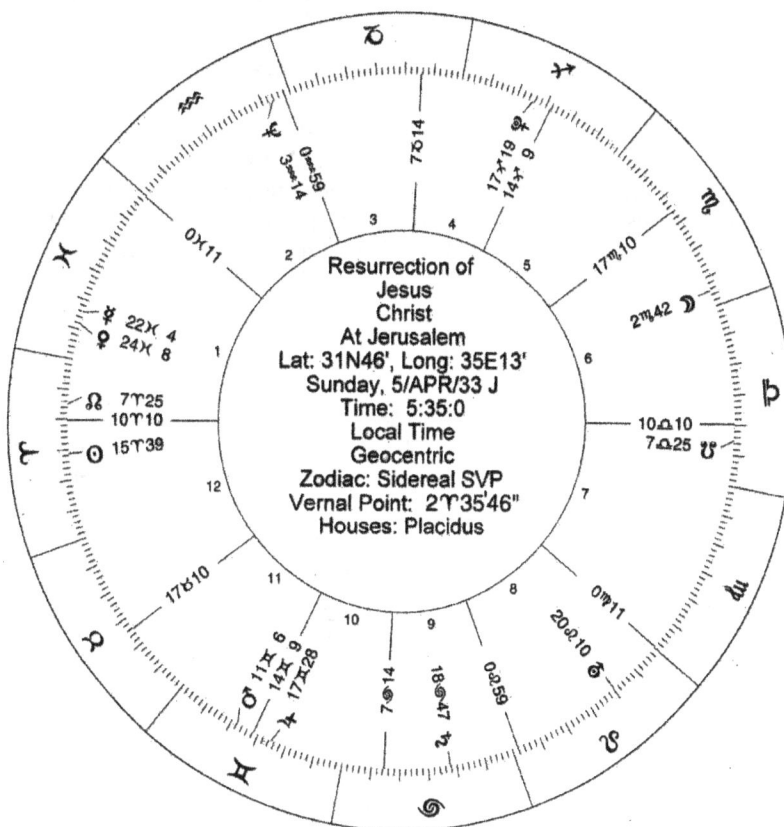

Resurrection of
Jesus
Christ
At Jerusalem
Lat: 31N46', Long: 35E13'
Sunday, 5/APR/33 J
Time: 5:35:0
Local Time
Geocentric
Zodiac: Sidereal SVP
Vernal Point: 2ϒ35'46"
Houses: Placidus

---

* The hermetic birth chart is computed on the basis of the astronomical system of the Danish astronomer Tycho Brahe (1546-1601) and is also referred to as the Tychonic chart.

Choreocosmos Experiences

For most of my adult life, I have had a habit of taking a pre-dawn walk or run at the time of the full Moon to some place where I have a clear view of the eastern and western horizons, so that I might stand between the disks of the rising Sun and the setting Moon. With my arms outstretched, it feels like I am holding these twin orbs in the palms of my hand, balancing and weighing them, and experiencing their raying forces within me.

Cosmic Dance affords this deep feeling of oneself as the microcosmic image of the Macrocosm, going beyond Sun and Moon to place into one's bones the other heavenly wanderers, set against the awesome canvas of the zodiacal constellations.

☆ ☆ ☆

At first, I am dancing, feeling the forms, the gestures, and the music, allowing them to work in me, and feeling them working in me. Then after a while, as I become more attuned, it is as if I am not dancing any more, but I am being danced! And sometimes I can even see that others in the circle are being danced too, because our movements are exactly synchronized, though perhaps not only in time – but in some element that I can almost see, and can certainly feel. It is as if we are moving in the same etheric current and are united in it. It is quite a joyful, peaceful experience.

Cosmic Dance balances me in the fullest way. It makes me feel more alive – more aware of others, including the beings in nature. The cosmic dances of Leo and the Sun are two of my favorites. Both of these enliven my heart, though each in its own way. My heart has softened, and opened. I see and feel more beauty in the world. I am more grateful, compassionate, and caring. But what is most intriguing is that it seems as though my body is full of wisdom and that the cosmic dances have put me in touch with that wisdom. I am able to understand things on deep levels; dormant capacities within me are awakening. But the ultimate gift of Cosmic and Sacred Dance, one that I have been given repeatedly by grace, is the experience of Divine Sophia. Her Grace, her Strength, her Wisdom, is the sweetest, most precious experience I could ever have. My faith is growing.

☆ ☆ ☆

I am not a dancer, and need help to remember forward/backward, right/left, and many other things! But after attending a Choreocosmos workshop given by Robert last summer, I couldn't stop dancing. Although at that workshop we had danced the planets in Libra, Scorpio and Sagittarius, I was drawn to the dance of the Sun in Gemini, which we had done in the workshop two years previously. I would take the opportunity when alone at home to push back the furniture and dance, sometimes several times a day - at times trying other dances, but always coming back to the Sun in Gemini - using a tape of the music (Pachelbel's Canon) or else in silence, recalling the music and imagining the whole dance as I danced the sign and the planet in turn. After about a week, as I danced, an unexpected and overwhelming feeling I have not experienced before came over me. It was as if my heart had softened and expanded, and I was enveloped in wave after wave of warmth and love. I sat down and gave myself up to experiencing this feeling, which must have lasted for several minutes. As the days passed, so did my need for this particular dance - but I believe I am beginning to have a new awareness, not only in myself, but also of the special nature of these cosmic dances.

☆ ☆ ☆

Choreocosmos

School of Cosmic and Sacred Dance

Cosmic and Sacred Dance is a schooling through music and movement, engaging the body, soul and spirit, with the intention of aligning oneself harmoniously with the spiritual-cosmic world. It leads to a living experience of the earth and cosmos expressed in the inner life of Nature (four elements), and through the movements of the planets against the background of the zodiac.

Cosmic dance (cosmic eurythmy) is a renewal of the ancient temple dances where the pupils were instructed in the mysteries of the elements relating to Mother Earth, then the mysteries of the planets in relation to the Cosmic Soul, and finally the mysteries of the zodiac pertaining to the World Spirit. *Introductory courses* of the School of Cosmic and Sacred Dance introduce these three levels of cosmic consciousness through the dances of the four elements, the seven planets, and the twelve signs of the zodiac, which correspond to the "body, soul, and spirit" of the human being. 12 + 7 + 4 = 23, signifying that there are 23 forms (choreographies), each with corresponding music and gestures, to be learnt as a foundation for cosmic dance. *Advanced courses* weave the dances of the planets and zodiac into a living experience of the cosmic tapestry of the heavens, bringing to expression the planets in relation to the zodiacal signs. This entails 84 possibilities (7 x 12 = 84) for the seven planets in each of the twelve signs of the zodiac. Through cosmic dance, it is possible to find a deeper relationship with the earth, the planets and the zodiac, and thus with Sophia – the Soul of the Cosmos. Cosmic eurythmy aspires to lead one to an experience of the Harmony of the Spheres, culminating in "cosmic communion".

Sacred dance (devotional eurythmy) is meditative movement to prayers and sacred texts. Through gestures and sacred forms, the heart's offering in prayer weaves an ethereal fabric between the individual and the spiritual world which sustains an inner field of spiritual activity. Sacred dance unites the soul of the individual with higher realms of consciousness through an expression of love offered through one's whole being. Sacred dance, whether done individually or in a group, serves to open one to spiritual and religious dimensions of experience.

Eurythmy: Alongside the words attributed to Apollo "Know thyself", Christ spoke the words "Heal thyself". A path toward self-healing can be found through the hidden power of gesture and sound – which form the basis of eurythmy. Eurythmy means "harmonious rhythm" and is applied therapeutically to healing through movement. The body, soul and spirit are harmonized through wisdom-filled eurythmy gestures.

Study and Ideal

In addition to cosmic and sacred dance, there is the study aspect of the schooling: entering into an understanding of the new star wisdom as belonging to the Mysteries of Sophia, the Divine Wisdom of the cosmos. The study activity entails learning about the planets, the signs of the zodiac, and the four elements (Fire, Air, Water and Earth). It also involves becoming acquainted with spiritual exercises – complementary to the cosmic and sacred dances – that can help open the way to knowledge and experience of the star mysteries of Divine Sophia.

Entering into these star mysteries, one comes to experience that there is a continual exchange of divine energy between the cosmos, the Sun and the Earth. This cosmic energy is Divine Love which weaves throughout the entire universe. The cultivation of love is the spiritual ideal of the School of Cosmic and Sacred Dance. In doing the cosmic and sacred dances, we seek to connect our hearts and minds with Divine Love and with the Supreme Consciousness that pervades all existence.

The Choreocosmos School of Cosmic and Sacred Dance, while based in America (under the auspices of the Sophia Foundation of North America), offers the training also in other countries. As a "moving school", with an underlying cosmic language as its basis, it seeks to be universal in scope. The stars belong to everyone and they are united with us all. Our image of the heavens is of a world working in beauty and divine harmony, and the more we enter into communion with the world of stars, the more our gestures and our whole lives begin to correspond to the harmony of the heavens. The cosmic dances, when moved in harmony, serve to create a vessel receiving higher spiritual impulses flowing down from the heavens into earthly life. At the same time, we learn through cosmic dance to "speak to the stars". This work can be seen as a spiritual training and discipline to take into one's daily life and practice. In due course of time it is anticipated that there will be an increasing number of qualified teachers of cosmic and sacred dance. For further information, please contact the Sophia Foundation of North America or visit the Sophia Foundation's website.

Lacquanna Paul

Lucky is a teacher of Qigong, the ancient Chinese form of healing movement. She is also a graduate of the Choreocosmos School of Cosmic and Sacred Dance and has discovered astonishing correspondences between the ancient healing art of Qigong and the modern healing movements of Eurythmy, both working with the flow of life force (*prana* or *chi*). Together with Robert, she has co-authored *Cosmic Dances of the Planets, Cosmic Dances of the Zodiac,* and *The Prayer Sequence in Sacred Dance.*

Robert Powell, Ph.D.

Robert is an internationally known lecturer, author, eurythmist and movement therapist. He is founder of the Choreocosmos School of Cosmic and Sacred Dance, and co-founder of the Sophia Foundation of North America. He received his doctorate for his thesis on the *History of the Zodiac,* now available as a book from Sophia Academic Press. His published works include: *The Sophia Teachings,* a six-tape series (Sounds True Recordings), as well as the following books: *Divine Sophia-Holy Wisdom, The Most Holy Trinosophia and the New Revelation of the Divine Feminine, The Sophia Teachings, Chronicle of the Living Christ, Christian Hermetic Astrology, The Christ Mystery, The Sign of the Son of Man in the Heavens, The Morning Meditation in Eurythmy,* and the yearly *Christian Star Calendar.* Robert teaches the cosmic dances of the planets and signs of the zodiac and facilitates sacred celebrations dedicated to the Divine Feminine. He offers workshops in Europe and North America, and leads pilgrimages to the world's sacred sites (1996 Turkey; 1997 Holy Land; 1998 France; 2000 Britain; 2002 Italy; 2004 Greece; 2006 Egypt; 2008 India).

Sophia Foundation of North America

Email: sophia@sophiafoundation.org
Website: www.sophiafoundation.org